The JAZZ Method for CLARINET

John O'Neill

Dedicated to Rafael Prieto,
a great musician and friend

SCHOTT
EDUCATIONAL
PUBLICATIONS

The *Jazz Method for Clarinet* can help students a great deal in many ways. There aren't many books in this area. I find this book contains a true method covering all the phases of the subject.

Jimmy Giuffre

Jimmy Giuffre

ACKNOWLEDGEMENTS

Many of the ideas in this book were inspired by four great teachers: Don Rendell, who took me under his wing when I was just beginning; Peter Ind, who introduced me to the concepts of Lennie Tristano and told me to listen to Pat Metheny; Lee Konitz, who gave me a new direction and discipline for my improvisation; and the late Warne Marsh.

I would also like to thank the following people:

Phil Lee, Jeff Clyne, Paul Clarvis and Jimmy Hastings for their superb musicianship, professionalism, patience and creative contribution during the recording of the accompaniments.

The staff at Schott & Co. Ltd.

All the musicians who gave permission for their compositions to be included in this book.

All my students, who played such an important part in shaping the book.

Nick Taylor of Porcupine Studio for his engineering and mixing.

Henry Binns for his photographs.

John Minnion for his line drawings.

Bob Glass of Ray's Jazz Shop for his help in compiling the discography.

Willie Garnett for looking after my instruments.

Rafael Prieto, 'mi hermano del alma', whose friendship and generous hospitality made it possible for me to 'recharge my batteries' and complete this project.

My family and friends for their unwavering support and belief.

British Library Cataloguing-in-Publication Data. A catalogue record for this book is available from the British Library

ISBN 0 946535 21 3

© 1993 Schott & Co. Ltd, London

Designed and typeset by Geoffrey Wadsley
Cover: Benny Goodman © Max Jones Files/Redferns, London

CONTENTS

The publishers would like to thank the following for allowing the use of their material in this publication:
John Minnion for the illustrations.
Henry Binns for the technical photographs.
Steve Berry, Dave Cliff, Tony Crowle, Ted Gioia, Jimmy Giuffre, Peter Hurt, Lee Konitz, Adrian Litvinoff, Roland Perrin and Don Rendell for their compositions.
Bocu Music Ltd, Ecaroh Music Inc., Marada Music Ltd and Prestige Music Ltd for their copyright music.

The author and publishers also wish to acknowledge, with thanks, Redferns Music Picture Library/Photographers: Max Jones Files (Johnny Dodds, p. 13; Artie Shaw, p. 13; Jimmy Hamilton, p. 13; The Count Basie Band, p. 21; Stan Getz with Benny Goodman, p. 27; Miles Davis, p. 39; John Coltrane, p. 55; Jimmy Giuffre, p. 71; Horace Silver, p. 74; Dave Brubeck Quartet, p. 86; Pee Wee Russell, p. 91), Charles Stewart (Eric Dolphy, p. 13), William Gottlieb (Louis Armstrong, p. 43; Thelonious Monk, p. 52; Charlie Parker, p. 69; Lester Young, p. 88), Tim Hall (Eddie Daniels, p. 90).
© Redferns, London

HOW TO USE THIS BOOK

Mastery of the foundation techniques presented in Part One is the key to playing the clarinet well, so please ensure you are comfortable with the exercises in this section of the book before attempting the pieces in Part Two.

Many of the chapters finish with suggestions for further listening, reading or practice. You are advised to adopt as many of these suggestions as possible in order to gain maximum benefit from the method.

If your speakers are connected properly the rhythm section will be heard from the left speaker and the clarinet from the right speaker. By using the 'balance' controls on your music system you will therefore be able to adjust the 'mix' between clarinet and rhythm section, or indeed to filter the clarinet out completely. This means you can choose to play with or without the clarinet for guidance. There are also several pieces which give you the further option of playing a duet part.

You should not expect to be able to play every piece immediately with the CD. It may require several hours of practice to work some of the music up to speed. If the music is too fast do not struggle to play with the recorded accompaniment—such practice is fruitless and frustrating. It is far better to practice **slowly**—at half-speed or even slower—and gradually build up to the challenge of playing with the CD.

It is particularly important that you develop your ear as well as your technique and ability to read. With this in mind try to play by ear as much as possible, for example by memorizing the tunes after you have learnt to read them or by transposing them into other keys or different registers of the instrument.

This book is not a rigid 'classical' method. Once you have learnt to play what is written you should feel free to alter rhythms, embellish or improvise. Many of the tunes will benefit from being treated in this way.

Above all ENJOY YOURSELF!

SOME THOUGHTS ABOUT PRACTICE

Try to make the environment you practise in as pleasant as possible. The room should be bright and well ventilated. It should also preferably be not too cluttered—if there is a lack of bare wall space the room will lack resonance and your sound will be deadened. Soft furnishings like thick carpets and curtains have a particularly muffling effect. On the other hand this might be an advantage if your neighbours complain about the noise!

It is very important to practise regularly—every day if possible. 20 minutes a day is much more valuable than one or two much longer sessions a week. If you practise more intensively remember that it is more effective to play for short periods of 20 minutes to half an hour with breaks in between than to play for hours at a stretch.

Do not expect to progress at a uniform rate, however hard you practise. The foundation techniques in particular can take a long time to master. Very often you will encounter the 'plateau effect', where you feel for a long time that you are not progressing at all. Do not be discouraged! Such periods are nearly always followed by a dramatic leap forward.

Avoid practising when you are tired. It may be more effective to practise at the beginning or middle of the day than at the end if your lifestyle permits.

Do not practise in a half-hearted way—you will be wasting your time.

Warm up properly—long notes or simple tonguing exercises are ideal.

You can do a lot of valuable practice without the instrument in your hands—singing, clapping or listening to music for example.

Avoid becoming obsessed by any one aspect of your playing—there are many different skills to acquire.

ABOUT THE CLARINET

Johann Christoph Denner of Nuremberg is generally given the credit for inventing the clarinet, at the beginning of the eighteenth century, although the earliest known instruments are by his son Jacob. It had become widespread by the 1780s, and was established as a virtuoso solo voice by Mozart in his Quintet and Concerto for clarinet, but it was not until the early part of the nineteenth century that the clarinet became a regular member of the orchestra. This was also the period when technical innovations by instrument makers began to transform the clarinet into an instrument which more closely resembles the modern one.

The frequent use of the clarinet in early jazz bands can probably be explained by the widespread availability of the instrument in New Orleans on account of the great tradition of marching bands there. Its typical role was to improvise a florid counter-melody while another instrument, usually the trumpet, played the tune. The playing of Johnny Dodds on the Hot Five and Hot Seven recordings of Louis Armstrong is a perfect example of this style. Many of the early players favoured clarinets with simpler fingering systems like the Albert system.

The clarinet was the main woodwind instrument in jazz until the 1930s, when the saxophone began to be preferred, probably because of its greater carrying power in the big bands which had begun to be so popular, and because emergent soloists like Coleman Hawkins and Lester Young found the saxophone to be technically less demanding and capable of a greater variety of tone colour. Since the late 1940s very few of the modernists have played clarinet, although there have been some noteworthy exceptions (like Buddy DeFranco, Art Pepper, Jimmy Giuffre, Phil Woods, Eddie Daniels and Anthony Braxton), and the instrument's popularity among players in the older New Orleans style has never waned.

There are many different types of clarinet including sopranino, soprano, alto, bass and contrabass, and orchestral players generally carry with them a clarinet pitched in A. The B♭ soprano clarinet has been the most widely used by jazz musicians, although many modern players have been fascinated by the mysterious timbre of the bass clarinet, the most influential exponent on this instrument being the late Eric Dolphy.

The most expensive professional instruments are made of wood, usually African blackwood, but the use of plastics has made possible the production of student instruments which are mechanically reliable, quite well in tune and reasonably priced.

Try to seek the advice of a teacher or professional player before buying an instrument. Second-hand instruments can sometimes represent excellent value but they need to be expertly assessed.

FURTHER STUDY

Reading:
JOACHIM E. BERENDT, *The Jazz Book*
BARRY KERNFELD, ed., *The New Grove Dictionary of Jazz*
STANLEY SADIE, ed., *The New Grove Dictionary of Music and Musicians*

Part One:
The Foundation Techniques

BREATHING EXERCISES

In clarinet playing the sound is produced by the breath passing across the reed and making it vibrate. Good breathing technique is therefore essential. The following exercises will help to develop this.

Stand in front of a mirror, preferably one in which you can see yourself from the waist up. Breathe in through the mouth. You may have raised the shoulders and lifted the chest to accomplish this. For the purposes of woodwind playing this is both unnecessary and incorrect. Nor is it how you breathe when you allow unconscious processes to take over.

Exercise 1

Take hold of an average sized hardback book, lie on the floor on your back, place the book on your abdomen and relax (Fig. 1). Do not try to breathe in any special way. Simply observe the natural breathing process. You will notice that the book rises as you breathe in and falls as you breathe out. In other words **expansion on inhaling, contraction on exhaling.**

Fig. 1

Now all you have to do is achieve this in a vertical rather than a horizontal position and as a slightly more controlled, conscious process.

Fig. 2

Fig. 3

Exercise 2

- Place the hands on the abdomen (Fig. 2).
- Breathe in through the mouth—a small sip of air rather than a massive gulp. The hands should be pushed out slightly. Exhale.
- Now place the hands on the back (Fig. 3). Breathe in again. You should notice that the hands are pushed backwards. It is as if you were breathing in through two holes in the back underneath the hands. The point is that you are not simply pushing the stomach out but achieving all-round expansion in the area of the waist and lower ribs.

This kind of breathing is called diaphragm breathing. The diaphragm is the powerful muscular floor to the chest cavity. In correct deep breathing the diaphragm moves down to make room as the lungs inflate, thus bringing about the expansion described.

You must now turn your attention to the exhalation. The diaphragm is like a piece of elastic. Left to its own devices it will simply spring back into position and the exhalation will be very short-lived. You might liken this effect to blowing up a balloon and then letting go of it. The balloon flies around the room and within seconds has emptied itself of air. If you let go of your breath in an uncontrolled way your note on the clarinet will be as erratic and short-lived as the flight of the balloon! You must exert a braking influence on the upward movement of the diaphragm, and do this by contracting the abdominal muscles.

Here is an exercise for practising abdominal control:

Exercise 3

- Breathe in (as described in Exercise 2 above).
- Now breathe out making a loud whispered 'ah' sound. Keep the throat open and relaxed. The 'ah' should be as long and steady as possible—ten or fifteen seconds would be reasonable for a beginner.

What you should notice is that the stomach muscles squeeze more and more firmly until the breath runs out. This effect can be likened to squeezing out a sponge. If you wish to achieve a steady flow of water you must squeeze first gently and then ever more tightly.

When putting the instrument together you should avoid exerting excessive pressure on the mechanism, since this might cause the keys or rods to bend. If any of the joints are stiff apply a little grease to the cork (see Appendix 4). Here is one way of assembling the instrument.

● Hold the lower joint in one hand, avoiding unnecessary contact with the key mechanism, and connect the bell by means of a twisting motion (see Fig. 4).

Fig. 4 *Connecting bell and lower joint*

● You can now hold the bell and lower joint without applying any pressure to the keys while you connect the top joint. **It is vital to depress the second ring key of the top joint otherwise the two parts of the 'correspondent' key mechanism may be damaged** (see Figs. 5 and 6). The upper and lower joints should be connected so that the ring keys are in line (see Fig. 7).

Fig. 6

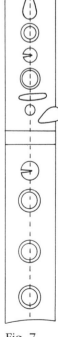

Fig. 5

Fig. 7

● Connect the barrel with the mouthpiece.

● You should now position the reed on the mouthpiece. Reeds must always be handled with great care since they are very delicate and easily damaged.

(i) First thoroughly moisten the reed by placing the blade or scraped out part in your mouth.

(ii) The flat part of the reed should now be placed on the mouthpiece table and positioned so that it is straight in relation to the mouthpiece rails (see Fig. 8). The tip of the reed should be level with the tip of the mouthpiece when viewed from sideways on (see Fig. 9). One millimetre too high or too low can make blowing much more difficult, so please take care.

(iii) The ligature should be slightly behind the blade of the reed and should be centralized (see Fig. 10). The screws should be done up until they are finger-tight, but no tighter. If the ligature is the correct size the screw threads will be visible between the lugs.

● Finally you should connect the mouthpiece and barrel with the rest of the instrument, ensuring that the reed is in line with the speaker key (see Fig. 10).

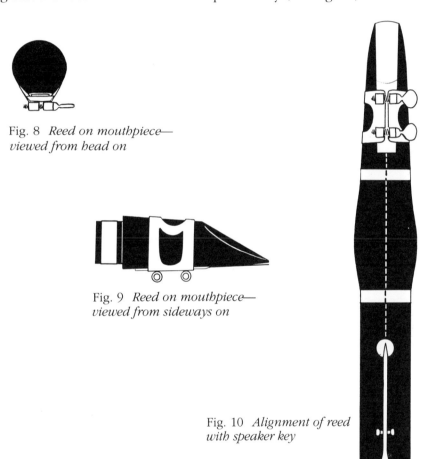

Fig. 8 *Reed on mouthpiece—viewed from head on*

Fig. 9 *Reed on mouthpiece—viewed from sideways on*

Fig. 10 *Alignment of reed with speaker key*

Tuning Position

The note B on the B♭ clarinet should correspond to A on a piano, tuning fork or pitch pipe. (An additional tuning note, concert D, is provided on the CD accompaniment so that—in the early stages—you can tune by fingering E.) If your note is too 'sharp' or high you will need to pull the barrel out from the top joint. You should not pull out more than about two millimetres—if the instrument is still sharp it is preferable from the point of view of its internal tuning to pull the top joint away from the lower joint.

If your note is too 'flat' or low this is more of a problem, since there is no quick way to make the instrument any shorter. Sometimes the tuning will correct itself as the instrument warms up—temperature changes can drastically affect tuning and the clarinet will be lower in pitch when cold. In other cases the flatness may be related to an incorrect embouchure (see p. 14). If difficulties persist it may be necessary to try a shorter barrel.

If you find that you are easily confused as to how pitch is affected by the tuning position remember that shorter tubes—e.g., trumpet—produce higher notes, while longer tubes—e.g., tuba—produce lower notes.

Disassembly

It is important to put the instrument back in its case after you have finished playing. If you leave it assembled for long periods the corks and/or tenons will wear and the instrument will get dirty and be exposed to the risk of accidental damage.

After you have finished playing you should clean out the inside of the instrument with a pull-through (see Appendix 4). Remove the reed, **gently** wipe off excess moisture, and clean out the inside of the mouthpiece with a tissue, taking great care not to rub too hard in the area of the baffle and mouthpiece tip. The reed should be stored in a reed guard (see Appendix 4) or replaced on the mouthpiece, but on no account left loose in the case. Remember to use the mouthpiece cap to protect the reed and mouthpiece tip.

POSTURE AND HAND POSITION

Good posture is vitally important in clarinet playing.

Stand with the feet about the same distance apart as your shoulders. Your weight should be evenly distributed over the soles of the feet. Imagine you are a puppet being lifted up towards the ceiling by a string attached to the crown of your head. This should induce a lengthening of the spine and neck and a general feeling of lightness. It will help you to keep the chest open and the shoulders relaxed if there is a space between the elbows and the sides of the body.

Fig. 11. *Posture: standing—front view*

Fig. 12 *Posture: standing—side view*

When sitting down you must keep the back straight. Do not slouch or slump.

Fig. 13 *Posture: sitting—side view*

The instrument should be held at an angle of between 30 and 40 degrees to the body. It is important to remember that you are not supposed to blow **down** the clarinet—the instrument comes into the mouth at an angle.

Feel free to move around while you are playing but try to return always to your position of equilibrium.

Traditionally, the weight of the instrument has been supported entirely on the top joint of the right thumb (see Fig. 14). However, a recent invention now makes it possible to use a neck-strap to assist in supporting the weight (see Appendix 4). This device is certainly worth investigating. Please do not resort to trying to provide additional support by placing the right forefinger under the side keys or by moving the thumb too far across. This is a common fault among beginners, particularly younger ones. If you find that the thumb gets tired you should practise in shorter spells, with frequent rests, until you have developed the necessary strength in the thumb to cope with longer sessions. The commercially available rubber pads which fit over the thumb rest offer a further means of easing strain on the thumb joint (see Appendix 4).

Fig. 14 *Correct position of right thumb*

● The fleshy pad at the end of the finger should make contact with the keys or tone holes (see Fig. 15). In the case of the open holes it is vital to ensure that air does not escape, since even the tiniest leaks can lead to squeaks or make the notes difficult to produce. However, do not press too hard, or you will lose the sensitivity in the finger-tips which is so essential for clean technique.

Fig. 15

● The fingers should be gently curved, not flat or contracted.
● The fingers move by means of a hammer action which is initiated at the knuckle joint. Movement of the other finger joints should be kept to a minimum.
● The fingers should stay as close as possible to the keys. Do not waste energy!
● In order for the fingers to stay relaxed and move efficiently it is necessary that the neck muscles, shoulder joints, elbows and wrists should also be relaxed.

TONE QUALITY

The quality of sound you produce on the clarinet will be greatly influenced by the sound that you hear in your head. In order to develop your concept of tone quality you should listen to the great exponents of your instrument as often as possible. Here is a list of some of the most influential clarinet players in the history of jazz. They have been loosely divided into stylistic categories, although it is important to understand that in many cases their careers span a number of styles:

New Orleans	Swing and Mainstream	Bebop, 'Cool' and West Coast	Contemporary and Avant Garde
Johnny Dodds	Benny Goodman	Jimmy Hamilton	Eric Dolphy
Jimmie Noone	Artie Shaw	Tony Scott	(bass clarinet)
Sidney Bechet	Bob Wilber	Buddy DeFranco	Eddie Daniels
George Lewis	Kenny Davern	John LaPorta	Anthony Braxton
Albert Nicholas		Jimmy Giuffre	(contrabass clarinet)
Edmond Hall			
Leon Roppolo			
Jimmy Dorsey			
Barney Bigard			
Pee Wee Russell			

Jimmy Hamilton

Artie Shaw

Johnny Dodds

Eric Dolphy

There have also been several players better known for their work on the saxophone who are also superb clarinet players. Lester Young (Swing), Art Pepper and Phil Woods (both bebop) are just three examples.

For some suggested recordings please consult the Discography (Appendix 2). You should also listen to players of other instruments whose sound you are attracted to, for example the trumpet sound of Louis Armstrong, Miles Davis or Chet Baker, or the saxophone sound of Ben Webster, Stan Getz or John Coltrane. Do not confine yourself to jazz! Remember Duke Ellington's words: 'There are only two kinds of music—good and bad'. You can improve your tone just as much by listening to a great opera singer like Luciano Pavarotti or a great string player like Jascha Heifetz.

THE EMBOUCHURE

- Place the top front teeth on the top of the mouthpiece, ensuring they are centralized. The exact distance from the tip of the mouthpiece will vary according to your 'bite' and the dimensions of the mouthpiece, and can only be established by trial and error. In order to exert maximum control over the vibrating length of the reed the lower lip should come into contact with the reed at the point where it meets the flat table of the mouthpiece. To achieve this, a person with 'overbite' (upper teeth that protrude significantly beyond the lower ones) will need to put more mouthpiece in the mouth than a person with normal bite. A mouthpiece with a longer 'lay' (see Appendix 3) will also require that the upper teeth are positioned further forward.
- The lower lip should be slightly turned in, about as much as if you were shaping to say the consonant 'f' or 'v'. Do not squeeze too hard. The clarinet embouchure is **firm but relaxed.**
- The corners of the mouth should be drawn slightly up and back towards the corners of the eyes. The effect of this movement is to activate the muscles of the lower lip and to stretch the area of skin between the lower lip and the chin.
- The lower jaw should be kept in a natural position. Do not exert pressure on the reed by biting or by thrusting the jaw forward.

FIRST ATTEMPTS

Finger the note E (see fingering diagram below—for basic fingering position see Fig. 15) and try to blow as long and steady a tone as possible. At this point many people forget what they have learnt about breathing. You must remember that the embouchure is only a funnel for the breath. It is vital to support the air column by contracting the stomach muscles (see Exercise 3 under Breathing Exercises, p. 7.)

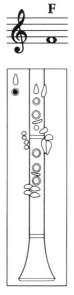
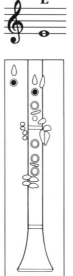
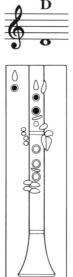
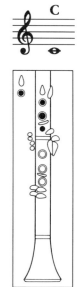

Your first week's practice should consist of ten to fifteen minutes a day—no more, no less—trying to get this E sounding as convincing as possible. For variety you may play F, D and C as well. This will be good preparation for your first tunes. Do not neglect this practice or feel that it must be got out of the way so you can get on to 'real music'. If you cannot sustain a steady tone on one note you will never be able to play a tune effectively.

It is a good idea to do your long-note practice in front of a mirror, which will provide a visual correlation for any changes in the sound and will enable you to check that you are not developing any of the faults listed below.

Common Embouchure Faults

- Corners of the mouth pointing down, leading to a weak and unsteady sound.
- Chin collapsing upwards towards the lip. This usually results in a feeble tone.
- Not enough mouthpiece in the mouth, producing a wavering and muffled sound.
- Too much mouthpiece in the mouth, producing a raucous tone.
- Not enough lip turned in, producing a loss of control.
- Too much lip turned in, also leading to a weak and unsteady sound.
- Thrusting the jaw forward, which can produce squeaks or a raucous sound.
- Cheeks puffing out, making it difficult to focus the breath.

TONGUING

Another vital foundation technique for playing the clarinet is tonguing. The tongue is the clarinettist's equivalent of a violin bow, or a drumstick. It allows you to start notes clearly and precisely, to repeat notes and to achieve all kinds of different phrasings and articulations.

Exercise 1

Imagine that you are a ventriloquist.* Sing any note that is comfortably within your voice range using the syllable 'doo'. Repeat the 'doo' sound slowly and in a steady rhythm using **one breath only**. You should produce a continuous sound as if you were singing one long note. Look at yourself in the mirror while doing this. There should be **no movement of lips, teeth or jaw**. Only the front part of the tongue moves. You will find that the tongue movements have to be very delicate to achieve this. It is also important that the tongue moves **straight up and down**.

Now you will try to apply this movement to the clarinet, using a stage-by-stage process. The following exercises should be practised in sequence.

* I am grateful to my first teacher Don Rendell for this exercise.

Exercise 2a
- Blow the note E and hold it steady for a few seconds.
- Move the tongue up to touch the edge of the reed only (Fig. 16) and hold it there for a few seconds, still maintaining breath pressure. Usually it will be just behind the tip of the tongue that makes contact with the reed, but if you have a larger or smaller tongue it may be more comfortable to touch the reed with a different part (Figs. 17 and 18). You should experience a kind of bottled-up sensation.
- Pull the mouthpiece out of the mouth. There should be a rush of air, rather like air being released from a tyre. If not, you are failing to maintain the pressure of air behind the tongue, which is vital for good tonguing.

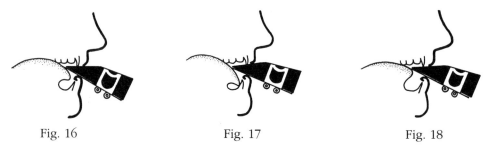

Fig. 16   Fig. 17   Fig. 18

Exercise 2b
- Blow the note E and hold it steady for a few seconds.
- Move the tongue up to the reed and hold it there for a few seconds.
- Move the tongue back down to its original position, slightly below the reed. The note should sound again immediately. If it does not you have probably forgotten about maintaining the breath pressure!

Exercise 2c
- Blow the note E and hold it steady for a few seconds.
- Move the tongue to the reed and then **immediately** down again. The tongue should move lightly and effortlessly, in much the same way as it did for Exercise 1. Listen to your sound. The action of the tongue should not disturb the tone quality in any way nor constrict the throat, which should be kept open and relaxed.

Exercise 3
You should now practise blowing a single note and tonguing at regular intervals, starting at speeds of about one note every four seconds. Slow practice is the key to mastering most things in music. It gives you plenty of time to become aware of what you are doing.

The Attack

For **starting** notes with the tongue the procedure is as follows:

1. Breathe in.
2. Set the embouchure and keep it **absolutely still**.
3. Move the tongue up to the reed in the manner already described.
4. Build up the air pressure just behind the tongue. You should experience the same bottled-up sensation described in Exercise 2a above. The stomach muscles should be firm, supporting the air column.
5. Move the tongue down. The note should sound immediately. You may find it helpful to imagine you are saying 'doo'.

Stopping the Note

The note is stopped by moving the tongue up to touch the edge of the reed. You will have to do this very gently to achieve a clean end to the note.

Some Common Faults

- Touching the underneath of the reed.
- Moving the tongue backwards and forwards rather than up and down.
- Moving the tongue too much.
- Moving the embouchure when you tongue, resulting in distortion of the tone.
- Not maintaining breath pressure.

Summary

- Just behind the tip of the tongue should touch only the edge of the reed.
- The tongue should move up and down (no more than about five millimetres in either direction.)
- Touch the reed as gently as possible. If you can touch it any more gently you are touching it too hard.
- Move the tongue as little as possible and keep it close to the edge of the reed.
- Keep the embouchure still.
- Maintain breath pressure.

During the second week you should first practise long notes and then the tonguing exercises.

You have now been taught the vital foundation techniques of the clarinet. Whatever kind of music you play these techniques for producing and articulating the sound will always be involved, so practise them diligently.

Part Two:
Playing the Music

CHAPTER 1

The Staff

Music is written on a staff (plural, staves), a group of five parallel lines.

Pitch, or how high or low a note is (see under Tuning Position, p. 9) is indicated by the position of that note on the staff—the higher the note the higher it is on the staff. Music uses a seven-letter alphabet from A to G to describe the pitch of notes:

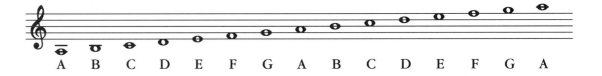

A   B   C   D   E   F   G   A   B   C   D   E   F   G   A

Do not worry about trying to memorize all these notes at once—you will only need to know four of them in order to play the pieces in the first two chapters.

Leger Lines

The extra lines written above and below the staff are known as leger lines.

Clefs

The sign at the beginning of the staff is a treble clef sign. The word clef is derived from the French word for a key. It shows the position of a particular note on the staff and thus is the key for finding the position of all the other notes. All clarinet music is written in the treble clef, a stylized form of the letter G, curling to indicate the position of that note.

Bars and Bar-Lines

Vertical lines written across the staff are bar-lines. The spaces between the bar-lines are called bars. Bars divide the music into easily recognizable units of time. They do not represent stops or pauses. They simply make counting easier, and counting, as you will see, is vital in the reading of music.

Time Signatures

If you look at the beginning of 'Blues for Beginners' (p. 20) you will see two numbers written one over the other. This is the time signature. It can be thought of as a fraction, the top figure or numerator telling us the number of beats in the bar and the bottom figure or denominator the kind of beat. In this case there are four **quarter** or **crotchet** beats in each bar.

Note Durations

The table below shows the note durations that you will encounter in your first pieces and exercises:

Symbol	British Term	American Term	Number of Beats to Count in 4/4 Time
♩ or ↑	Crotchet	Quarter Note	One
♩ or ↑	Minim	Half Note	Two
o	Semibreve	Whole Note	Four

Pulse and Rhythm

Look at 'Blues for Beginners'. Count in groups of four beats and clap on every first beat, holding the hands together to express the duration of the semibreve,* which is four beats.

```
clap:  x           x           x           x
count: 1  2  3  4   1  2  3  4   1  2  3  4   1  2  3  4, etc.
```

What you are doing is counting the **pulse** and clapping the **rhythm**.

Rhythm is the organization of notes in time and is not **necessarily** regular, although in this instance it is. Pulse—often referred to as 'the beat'—is usually felt rather than heard and is nearly always regular. It is very often what we dance to in music. Pulse determines the speed of the music and helps us to measure the distance between notes.

Now you should practise counting and clapping with the CD accompaniment to 'Blues for Beginners'. The claps should coincide precisely with the notes of the clarinet. This procedure of counting and clapping before playing should be carefully adhered to throughout the book. Rhythm is the most basic element of music, and it is vital to master this aspect of each piece before proceeding further.

Taking a Breath

The commas written above the stave are suggested breathing places. Breaths should not be taken where doing so would destroy the flow of the music. There is a parallel here with speech, where breaths are generally taken at the end of sentences or phrases, except by small children who are still learning the art!

In 'Blues for Beginners' there are no spaces between the notes. In such cases you must create a breathing space by cutting the note before the breath mark slightly short. You should take small sips of air at regular intervals. Most beginners drastically overestimate the amount of breath they need—small amounts will be sufficient provided that the breath is adequately supported by the stomach muscles. Leave the top teeth where they are and inhale either through the mouth corners or by dropping the lower jaw. **Do not breathe through your nose!**

The following exercise may help you to become accustomed to the correct mode of breathing. Breathe at the commas. The rhythm should be regular and undisturbed by the taking of the breath. Count slowly and steadily.

Count aloud: 1 2 3 4 1 2 3 4 ' 1 2 3 4 1 2 3 4 ', etc.

Metronome Markings

Now you are ready to play 'Blues for Beginners'. The instruction ♩ = 90 at the beginning of the piece is a metronome marking, meaning that the music is to be played at a

---

* Claps can only indicate the position of notes in time—not their duration.

speed of around 90 beats per minute. A metronome is a device which marks the pulse by means of a regular click and would be a worthwhile purchase (see Appendix 4). Fingering positions for the pieces in this chapter and the following one are shown in the diagrams on p. 14.

2* **Blues for Beginners****

Chord progressions in **concert** pitch for this and all other tunes in the book can be found in Appendix 8.

Rests

'A la Mode' and 'Progression' introduce minims, and minim and semibreve rests. A minim is worth two beats in 4/4 time. The minim rest sits on the third line, measuring from the bottom of the staff upwards, and represents two beats of silence, while the semibreve rest hangs from the fourth line, representing four beats of silence. Silence in music is just as important as sound, so make sure you count the rests carefully.

There is an optional lower part to 'A la Mode', which can be played by a teacher or more advanced player.

3 **A la Mode**

* These numbers refer to tracks on the CD.

** All pieces are by John O'Neill unless otherwise indicated.

Repeats

At the end of 'Progression' is a double bar preceded by two dots. This means that you repeat from the beginning. There is only one repeat unless otherwise indicated.

CHAPTER 2

Riffs

'Out for the Count' is a twelve-bar blues consisting of a single phrase which is repeated three times. Short repeated phrases of this type are know as riffs. They were often used by big bands during the swing era as a means of building excitement, with different riffs sometimes being assigned to each section of the band. The Count Basie band of the 1930s is a perfect example.

The Count Basie Band

Crotchets

This is the first piece to use crotchets, which are worth one beat each in 4/4 time.

The 'Pick-Up'

You will notice that there are just two crotchets before the first bar line, in spite of the fact that the time signature indicates four beats to each bar. These two crotchets are an example of an **anacrusis**, sometimes referred to by jazz musicians as a 'pick-up'. An anacrusis is an unstressed note or group of notes at the beginning of a musical phrase. In this instance, the first strong accent falls on the F and not the C or D. Because of the anacrusis, there are only two beats rest in the bar before the repeat.

Out for the Count

5

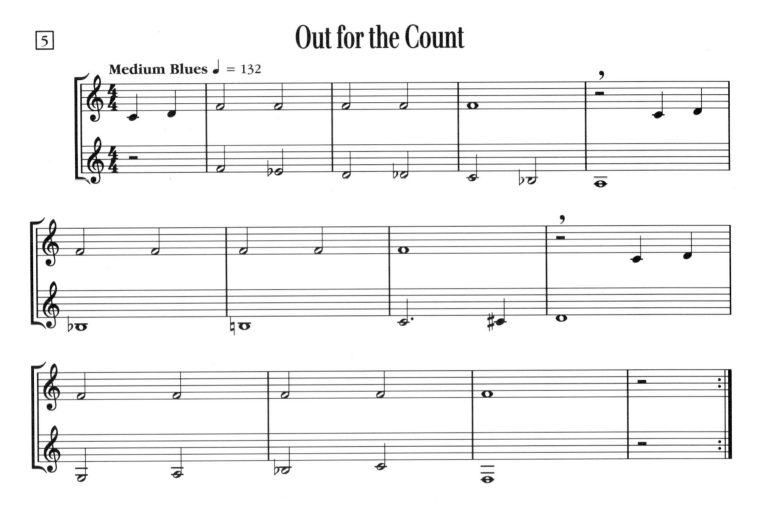

Slurs

The curved lines below the notes in 'P.M.' are **slurs**. You should tongue only the first note within a slur group. For example, in bar 1 you tongue the E but not the F.

P.M.

6

7

Third Attempt

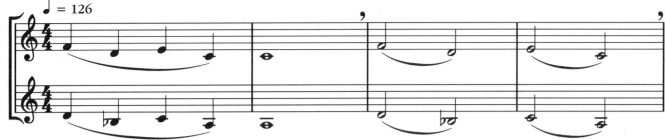

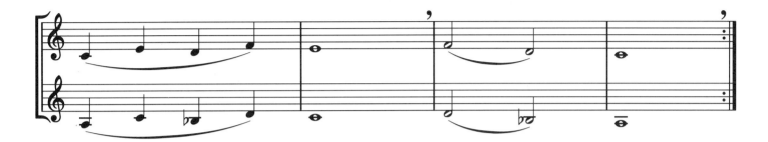

FURTHER STUDY

Listening:

COUNT BASIE, 'Jumping at the Woodside' from *Swinging the Blues.* A classic example of the use of riffs.

CHAPTER **3**

The four tunes in this section contain two new notes—low B and A.

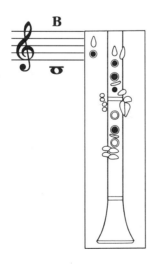
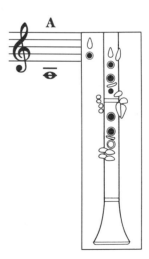

Dynamic Markings

The pieces in this chapter introduce dynamic markings. These are abbreviations of Italian words and are used to indicate volume levels. Here are some of those most commonly used:

Marking	Italian word	Meaning
pp	*pianissimo*	very quiet
p	*piano*	quiet
mp	*mezzopiano*	medium quite
mf	*mezzoforte*	medium loud
f	*forte*	loud
ff	*fortissimo*	very loud

Changes in volume on the clarinet are effected by varying the speed of the air flow by contracting the stomach muscles to a greater or lesser extent—the faster the air stream moves the louder the note. Paradoxically this means that to play quieter you need to work harder at contracting the stomach muscles. The following exercise is excellent for practising control of dynamics. Try to make sure that each note begins and ends at the same volume and that you achieve six distinct dynamic levels. You can play this exercise using any of the notes you have learnt so far.

The Pause

The sign ⌢ is a **pause**, sometimes called a *fermata*, which has the effect of prolonging the note beyond its written value, at the discretion of the performer or musical director. In the exercise you should therefore pause on each note that you play.

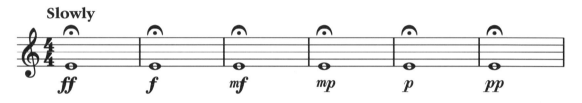

The sign 𝄥 at the beginning of 'South View' means that you remain silent for eight bars. Count carefully so that you know exactly when to come in. After that, there is a double bar with two dots placed **after** it. This is an indication of where you repeat **from**.

South View

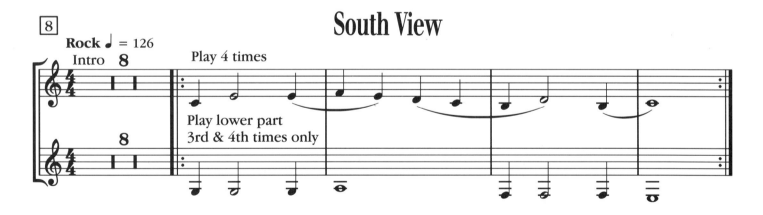

Ties

In 'Home Bass' you will notice that the C at the end of the first full bar is connected to the C at the beginning of the following bar by a curved line. This is called a **tie**. It has the effect of joining the two notes together as one, so you do not tongue the second C, but simply extend the first note by two extra beats. Do not confuse ties with slurs. A tie always connects notes of the same pitch, whereas a slur connects notes of different pitch.

The dynamic marking **p-mf** means you should play quietly the first time and mezzo-forte on the repeat. A similar principle applies with the marking **mp-f**.

Home Bass

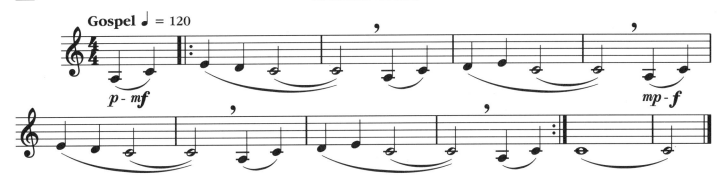

Dotted Notes

The fourth note of 'Los Azules' is a minim with a dot placed after it. A dot placed after a note extends its duration by half as much again. A dotted minim is therefore worth three beats (2 + 1).

Los Azules

FURTHER STUDY

It is important that you spend some of your practice time playing by ear. Try to memorize some of the tunes you have learnt so far and play them without the music. Inventing your own tunes would also be a good idea.

CHAPTER

Sharps, Semitones and Accidentals

In 'James' you will find F sharp for the first time. This note is indicated by a **sharp** sign ♯ written in front of the F. A sharp means the note is raised by one **semitone**, which is the distance between one note and its nearest neighbour note, i.e. the smallest interval 'officially' recognized in the mainstream of Western music. Signs which alter notes in this way are called **accidentals**. Accidentals affect every note of the same pitch in the bar, so in bar 3 of 'James' **both** F's are sharp.

This tune is an example of the bossa-nova rhythm, made famous in jazz by the early sixties recordings of tenor saxophonist Stan Getz.

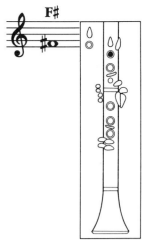

Flats

In 'Flat 5' the flat sign ♭ is introduced. When placed before a note as an accidental it means that the note is to be played a semitone lower.

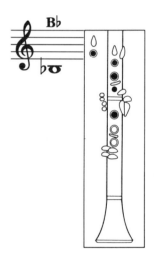

Crotchet Rests

The sign 𝄽 in 'Flat 5' is a crotchet or quarter-note rest. It represents one beat of silence in 4/4 time.

The Natural Sign

In 'Minor Problem' the second note of bars 1, 3 and 5 is preceded by another kind of accidental, the **natural** sign, which cancels any previous accidentals in the bar.

13

Minor Problem

Medium Groove ♩ = 126

FURTHER STUDY

Listening:

STAN GETZ, *Jazz Samba; Stan Getz and Joao Gilberto.* Both of these records are classic examples of the use of the bossa nova rhythm in jazz.

Stan Getz with Benny Goodman

CHAPTER **5**

The 'Throat' Register

Up until now you have been playing in the 'chalumeau' or lowest register of the clarinet. The chalumeau was a simple single-reed pipe which was an early ancestor of the clarinet. The pieces in this chapter introduce the notes between the G on the second line and B♭ on the middle line of the staff, which form the 'throat' register of the clarinet.

Enharmonic Notes

The note in between G and A is both one semitone higher than G (G♯) and one semitone lower than A (A♭). Notes like G♯ and A♭ which can be named in two different ways are said to be **enharmonic notes**. It is essential that you learn to think of these notes in both ways.

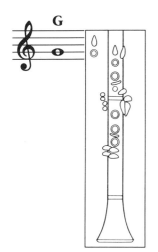 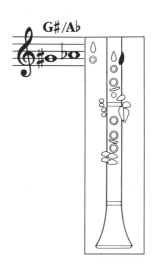 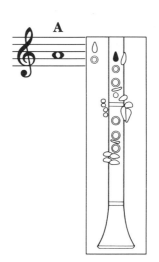 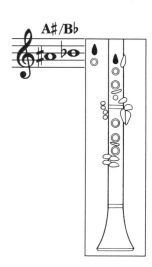

These notes have a thinner and sometimes more muffled tone quality than the notes you have played so far. You should not try to compensate for this by squeezing tighter with the mouth, since this will only make the problem worse. Indeed, excessive pressure on the underneath of the reed in the throat register often produces squeaks. Instead you should concentrate on keeping your throat open and relaxed and on supporting the air column by contracting the stomach muscles. You will eventually learn to 'humour' these notes and achieve a good tone from them.

The notes G♯, A and B♭ also present fingering problems. As you will see from the photographs, in the case of both the A key and the B♭ or 'speaker' key the **edge** of the finger and not the fleshy pad should make contact with the very edge of the key. The index finger and thumb should **roll** onto their respective keys and not lift or slide. As with all finger movements it is essential to keep the whole arm relaxed, and in particular the wrist. Where the index finger is concerned it may help you to think of clockwise movement of the hand proceeding from the forearm, as if you were turning a dial, or moving your wrist to look at the time on your watch.

Fig. 20
Fingering position for throat A♯/B♭

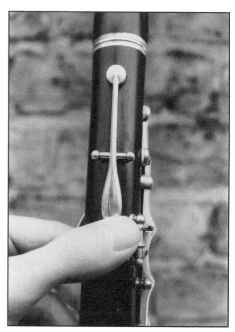

Fig. 19
Fingering position for throat G♯/A♭

Fig. 21
Thumb position for throat A♯/B♭

Mastering the technical problems presented by these notes is crucial, not least because it will help you to deal with other fingering difficulties which you will meet with later on, such as crossing the break (see Chapter 13). The following exercises have been designed to help you in this. Begin by playing them slowly and then gradually increase the metronome speed.

Sylvie's Dance

14

Accents

'K.O' introduces **accents**. The sign ∧ over the first note is a short accent, meaning that the note is to be attacked hard and then stopped short of its full written value.* The sign > below the second note means that the beginning of the note should be played with extra emphasis. This is achieved by a slight 'kick' of the stomach muscles, similar to what happens when you cough.

* Note for teachers: this is not the same as the classical staccato, which is lighter and shorter.

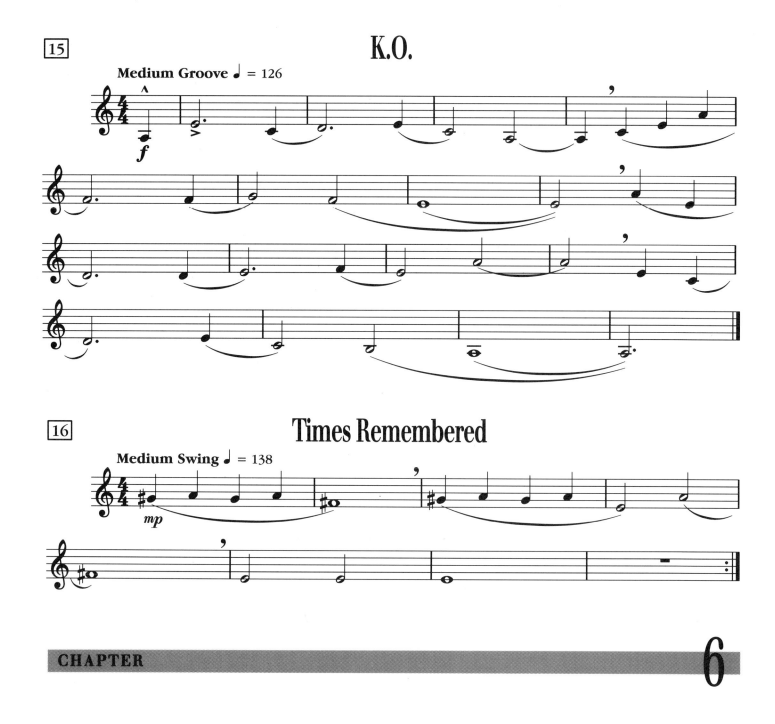

K.O.

15

Medium Groove ♩ = 126

Times Remembered

16

Medium Swing ♩ = 138

CHAPTER 6

The next two pieces introduce low G, F and E. These notes should not be difficult to produce provided that you are covering the holes properly with the fingers (see

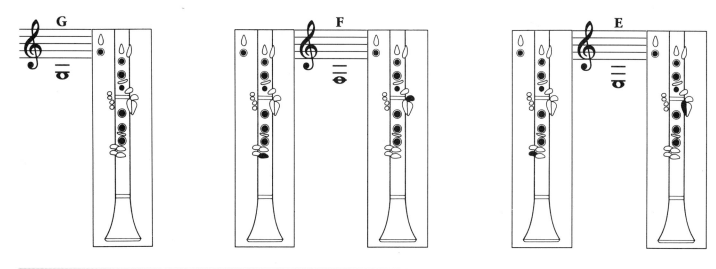

Fingering, p. 12). If, having checked that air is not escaping from underneath your fingers, you still experience problems, you should have your instrument examined by your teacher, a woodwind repairer, or another experienced player.

You should ensure that you are able to play these and any other pieces involving low F and E using either fingering possibility—e.g., right-hand little finger F followed by left-hand little finger E, and left-hand F followed by right-hand E in bars 6 and 7 of 'Interstellar'—since you will later encounter musical situations in which you do not have the luxury of a choice.

It is also important to note that the left- or right-hand little finger low F key can be held down when playing low E. This means that it is superfluous to lift the little finger when moving from F to E in 'Interstellar'.

Interstellar

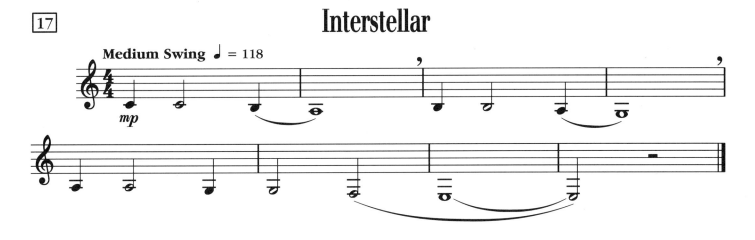

Syncopation

'251' is made more difficult by the presence of **syncopation**, which can be defined as the placing of accents where you would not normally expect to find them—the effect being one of rhythmic surprise. Much of the vitality of jazz derives from the extensive use of syncopated rhythms. In this example it is the fourth beats of the first, third and fifth bars which are syncopated.

251

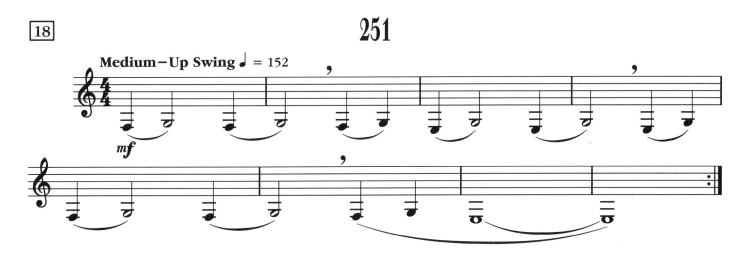

It would be good practice to try playing this tune starting on first space F.

FURTHER STUDY
Playing:
Play 'Blues for Beginners' from Chapter 1 again, but this time using low E and F.

Blue Jean

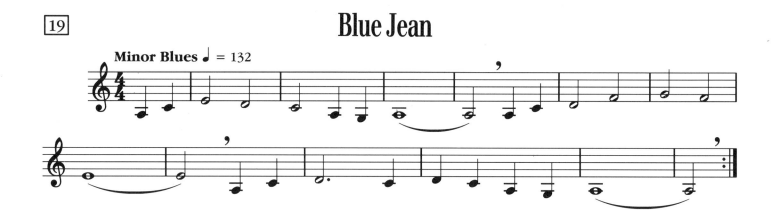

Improvisation

After you have played the tune of 'Blue Jean' try improvising with the accompaniment, using the following five notes:

It would be a good idea to learn these notes by heart before attempting to improvise.

During this improvised section you may play whatever you feel using these notes only. You can play the notes in any register, so you can also play low G and E and throat A. You need not worry about playing any 'wrong' notes, since all of these notes will sound fine wherever you play them.

Most beginner improvisers make the mistake of neglecting the rhythmic aspect of their playing. The following exercises should help with this problem:

● Clap out a solo, or tap one out on your legs or on a table top. Be as adventurous as you like, but try to maintain a strong rhythmic feeling in what you do, like a good jazz drummer.

● Once you are happy about clapping a solo return to the clarinet and try improvising again but this time think of the scale as a set of 'tuned drums', trying to retain the strong rhythmic feeling you had while you were clapping.

This exercise should have helped you to realize that the **most important element of any jazz solo is rhythm.**

Scales

The word scale is derived from the Italian *scala* meaning 'staircase' or 'ladder'. It is a series of single notes moving up or down in steps.

Chords

A **chord** is a combination of notes sounding together. Simple three-note chords are known as **triads**.

It is impossible to play chords on the clarinet in the way that a keyboard player or guitarist can, although some players have experimented with **multiphonics**—the playing of more than one note by use of alternative fingerings and advanced blowing techniques.

Arpeggios

An arpeggio is a chord played **melodically**, sounding the notes one after the other, rather than **harmonically**, playing the notes simultaneously.

Scales and arpeggios are the 'nuts and bolts' of most jazz improvisation, although to achieve good results creative rather than mechanical use must be made of them! Below are the F major scale and arpeggio.* They should be committed to memory and played slowly, gradually increasing the speed as your technique develops. Strive for rhythmic and tonal evenness. Scales and arpeggios should initially be played slurred to develop smooth technique. Once this has been mastered they may be tongued as well.

Once you are feeling comfortable with the scale and arpeggio try playing them with track [20] on the CD. When you can manage this you should begin to improvise using the scale notes.

* The construction of major and minor scales and arpeggios will be discussed at greater length in Chapter 17, p. 58.

The next two pieces introduce E♭ (whose enharmonic equivalent is D♯). The fingering charts show three different ways of playing this note. You should think of side E♭ as your basic fingering, but the '1-4' and '1-5' are useful alternatives, particularly when moving from B♭, or B, e.g. in bars 2 and 3 of 'Romancing'. If there is a choice between 1-4 and 1-5, e.g. when moving from E to E♭ and back again, you should choose 1-5, since the tone quality is noticeably better on most clarinets.

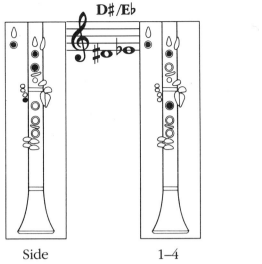
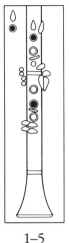

Side   1–4   1–5

Fig. 22 *Fingering position for side D♯/E♭*

Key Signatures

When accidentals are placed after the clef sign as in 'Roberto' they form a **key signature**, which tells you which notes are to be played sharp or flat for the duration of the entire piece rather than just for a single bar. In this case the placement of the flat signs mean that all B's and E's are to be played flat unless otherwise indicated by an accidental.

Roberto

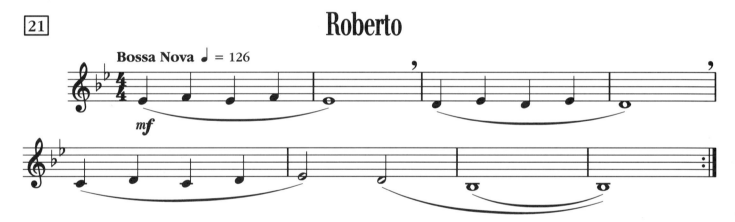

In the next piece the note G♭ is enharmonically equivalent to F♯.

D.S. al Coda

The term *D.S. al Coda*, an abbreviation of *Dal Segno al Coda*, means literally 'from the sign to the tail'. A coda is an extra section which is added to a piece. When you meet this instruction you repeat from the sign 𝄋 and then go to the coda at the coda sign 𝄌.

From this tune onwards detailed indications of where and how to tongue (articulation markings) have been omitted. You should experiment with many different possibilities for phrasing and expression, marking them in your copy with a soft pencil so that they can easily be altered. The following points may help to guide you:

● The first note of any new phrase should nearly always be tongued.
● Tongue only those notes which require extra emphasis.
● Avoid 'phrasing to the bar line' or tonguing the first beat of every bar. This kind of phrasing is particularly inappropriate to jazz.
● How to articulate a passage is often a matter of individual taste. There is more than one 'right' way.
● You will learn a lot by listening carefully to the example on the CD and to the recordings of great jazz players. Jazz is a language that is often best learnt by imitation.

Romancing

Medium Swing ♩ = 132

D.S. al Coda

CODA

Relative Keys

Below are the scales and arpeggios of B♭ major and G minor. You will notice that they share the same key signature. They are known as relative keys. They contain the same notes, except the seventh note of the G minor scale is sharpened, shown as required by an accidental and not in the key signature. There are various forms of the minor scale, this particular one being known as the harmonic minor. Do not skip scale practice. Its importance will become more apparent as you progress through the book. If you wish to become a good improviser knowledge of major and minor scales and arpeggios is vital. Remember, they should be committed to memory.

You may notice that the key signature for the B♭ major scale is the same as for the two pieces in this chapter, both of which are in the key of B♭ major. In other words, B♭ is the note towards which both these pieces gravitate—a kind of 'home base'. Songs written in major keys tend to be brighter or happier in mood, while songs in minor keys are generally more intense or sad.

B♭ major

You can practise improvising with the B♭ major scale using track [23] on the CD.

G minor

Below are fingering diagrams for three new notes and one alternative fingering.

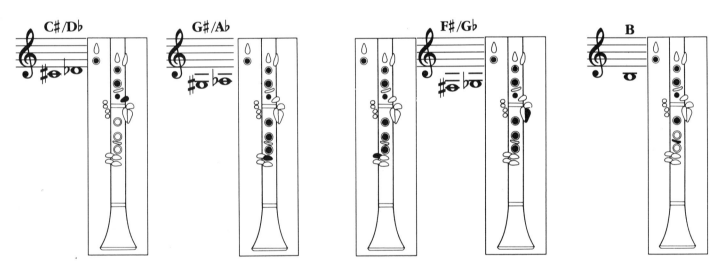

C♯/D♭ is another example of an enharmonic note.

The fingering exercises below are designed to give you practice in coordinating the movement of the third and fourth fingers:

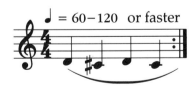

'Bird Waltz' is a blues inspired by the music of Charlie Parker (1920-1955), sometimes known as 'Bird'. Arguably the greatest of all alto saxophone players, he was one of the creators of Bebop, a jazz style which dominated the 1940s, and has continued to exert a powerful influence on contemporary music.

3/4 Time

This tune introduces 3/4 or waltz time, in which there are three crotchet beats to each bar. 3/4 time was rarely heard in jazz before the 1950s. It has become much more popular since then, and is particularly associated with the music of the lyrical and highly influential pianist Bill Evans.

In this and subsequent pieces 'L' and 'R' are used to indicate use of the left- and right-hand little finger.

Bird Waltz

Crescendo and Decrescendo

When it is wished to indicate that the music should gradually get louder or softer this can be done in two ways: either by writing *cresc.* or *decresc.* (Italian = *crescendo* or *decrescendo*, meaning getting louder or softer); or by the signs ⸺◁ and ▷⸺.
To practise this try the following exercise, using other notes for variation:

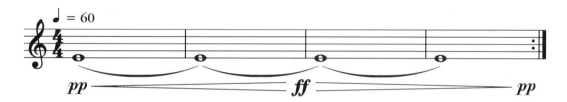

The lines under the notes in bars 9 and 10 of 'Devil Music' are tenuto marks, meaning these notes are to be held for their full value and connected as smoothly as possible.

Devil Music

'Apologies to Daisy' introduces **first and second time bars.** The second time bars are played as an **alternative**—never in addition—to the first time bars on the repeat.

The sign ✗ at the end indicates a whole-bar repeat.

Apologies to Daisy

Steve Berry

Use of Space

Make sure you do not clutter your solos with too many notes. The best jazz musicians know how to make effective use of **space**. There are two ways of creating space in a solo—one is by using silence and the other is by playing notes of longer duration. In either case you will find you have more time to be aware of what you and—just as importantly—the other musicians are doing. As a result your playing should become more relaxed, expressive and coherent. Trumpeter Miles Davis is a fine example of someone who uses space quite brilliantly.

Chromatic Scale

Now that you have learnt C♯/D♭ and low F♯/G♭ you are able to practise the **chromatic scale**, in which one moves by semitone steps from any note to the same note in the next register. The examples below show chromatic scales starting on E and B♭. In order to give you more practice with enharmonic notes I have written sharps in the ascending versions and flats in the descending versions of the scales. When playing these scales you will probably find it easier to use the alternative fingering for B shown at the beginning of the chapter.

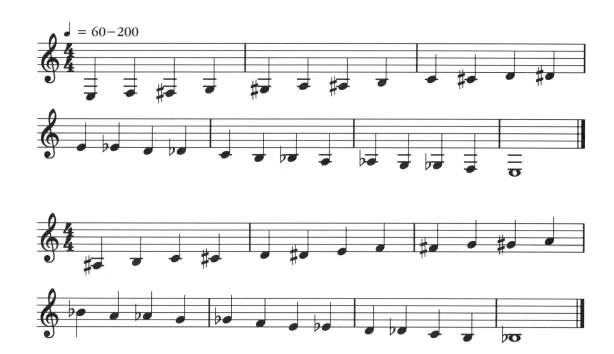

♩ = 60–200

FURTHER STUDY

Listening:

CHARLIE PARKER, 'Blues for Alice' from *Charles Parker* (Compact Jazz series).

BILL EVANS, 'Waltz for Debbie', from *At the Village Vanguard*. A beautiful example of a jazz waltz.

MILES DAVIS, *Kind of Blue*. Listen in particular to the trumpet solos for examples of the use of space.

Reading:

ROSS RUSSELL, *Bird Lives*.

GARY GIDDINS, *Celebrating Bird: The Triumph of Charlie Parker*.

ROBERT REISNER, *Bird: The Legend of Charlie Parker*.

Viewing:

'Bird' directed by Clint Eastwood.

Miles Davis

CHAPTER 11

Sight-reading is only one of the many skills a good jazz musician must acquire. A discriminating ear is possibly the most vital asset, since effective improvisation depends on being able to translate the ideas in your head onto the instrument as quickly as possible.

Ear Training

A lucky minority seem to develop fantastic aural perception at a very early age. At the other end of the spectrum true 'tone-deafness' is much rarer than people imagine. For the vast majority in between these extremes aural training can produce remarkable results.

Intervals

One important skill is the ability to recognize and sing intervals. Intervals are a means of expressing the distance between one note and another. You should begin to develop your sense of this by learning to sing the intervals of the major and minor scales. The chart below indicates the names of these intervals in the major scale, measuring them from the first note, also known as the **tonic**. The subsequent degrees of the scale are expressed as Roman numerals:

Major Scale (G)

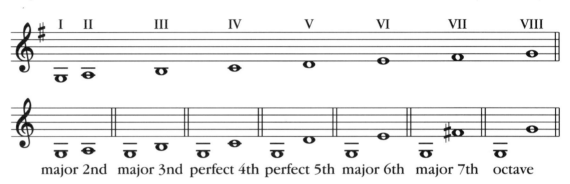

Harmonic Minor Scale (G)

The intervals between successive degrees of the harmonic minor scale and the tonic are the same, except I-III (which is a minor third) and I-VI (a minor sixth); these two intervals are a semitone smaller than their major counterparts:

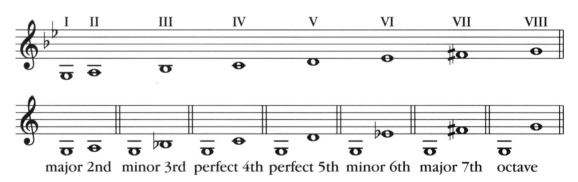

It is important to realize that the intervals are the same for every key. Thus, the distance between the tonic and the fifth note of any major or minor scale, measured as an ascending interval, is always a perfect fifth.

In the exercises which follow try not to be too self-conscious about your singing. Accuracy of pitch is more important than tone quality. Singing will help your clarinet playing and vice-versa—the technique of supporting the breath and relaxing the throat is almost identical.

Some intervals are much harder to sing than others. It is best to begin with trying to recognize and sing the ascending intervals.

Once you are confident with fifths you can progress to other intervals. A recommended order of study is: perfect fifth, perfect fourth, octave, major second, major third, minor third, major sixth, minor sixth, major seventh.

Some students find it helpful to use mnemonics for the intervals. For example, the first two notes of 'Oh When the Saints Go Marching In' are a major third apart. Some other possibly helpful mnemonics are 'Here Comes the Bride' for a perfect fourth, 'Twinkle Twinkle Little Star' for a perfect fifth and 'My Bonny Lies Over the Ocean' for a major sixth. You might wish to substitute some tunes of your own—the more familiar the better.

Having developed an ability to sing ascending intervals, you should next practise descending intervals. These are named in the major and harmonic minor scales as follows:

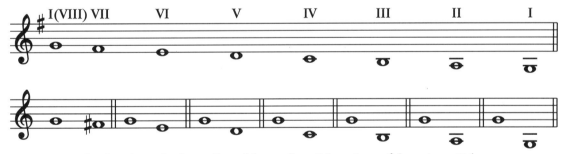

minor 2nd minor 3rd perfect 4th perfect 5th minor 6th minor 7th octave

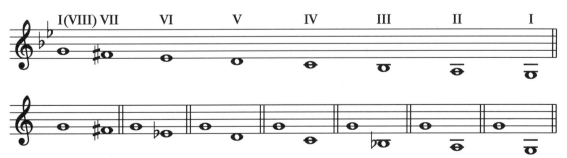

minor 2nd major 3rd perfect 4th perfect 5th major 6th minor 7th octave

Inversions

The interval which measures the distance between the same pair of named notes but in the opposite direction, e.g. from G **down** to A rather than **up** to A (or from G **up** to D instead of **down** to D) is known as an **inversion**. From the above examples you can see that the original interval and its inversion always add up to nine, e.g., seconds become sevenths and fourths become fifths; major intervals become minor when inverted and minor intervals become major; perfect intervals remain perfect.

You should practise singing descending intervals by adapting the exercises given above. A suggested order of study is: perfect fourth, octave, minor third, minor second, perfect fifth, major third, minor sixth, major sixth, minor seventh.

Playing by Ear

Playing by ear is one of the most enjoyable and effective ways of improving your aural perception. Any material will do—nursery rhymes, hymns, folk tunes, songs you hear on the radio, T.V. themes, advertising jingles—but the most relevant exercise would be to get hold of jazz recordings and learn to play jazz tunes. You will also develop your sound, sense of time and phrasing by listening to the jazz masters in this way.

If you cannot afford to buy the records, visit your local music library, which will often contain an excellent record collection. This is a good way to become familiar with the jazz heritage. You should start with simple melodies. Recordings by singers, for example the 1950s recordings of Frank Sinatra, are also good source material.

Proceed as follows:

1. Play the recording several times.
2. Sing the melody with the recording, trying to imitate as closely as possible with your voice the inflections of the instrument or voice. This technique of imitating instrumental sounds with the voice is known as scat-singing. Louis Armstrong, Ella Fitzgerald, Chet Baker, Al Jarreau and Bobby McFerrin are five of the very best scat-singers.
3. Sing the melody without the recording—this is much harder!
4. Play the melody with the recording. This will develop the ability to translate what you hear in your head to your fingers—a vital skill for musicians who wish to improvise.
5. Play the melody without the recording.

You may find this difficult at first but please persevere—it becomes easier with practice. This sort of exercise will develop your playing considerably.

Later on you can progress to more intricate melodies and even jazz solos. Some sort of device for slowing the music down to half-speed is invaluable. This could be either a reel-to-reel tape-recorder which records at both $7^1/2$ and $3^3/4$ ips or a record player which slows down to 16 rpm, preferably with sliding pitch control to facilitate tuning. Cassette players with slow-down facility are also available. These items can be relatively cheaply acquired through small-ad pages of newspapers, junk shops or second-hand audio equipment shops. The ability to slow down solos opens up a whole world of difficult music to your ears. Charlie Parker is said to have used this method to study the music of his idol Lester Young.

FURTHER STUDY

Playing:

This game can be played with your teacher or another clarinettist: position yourselves so that neither player can see the other's fingerings, and take it in turns to sound any note. The other player must try to sound the same note in response. By practising regularly at this game you will be surprised how easy it becomes to find the correct note on the first attempt.

Reading:

PAUL HINDEMITH, *Elementary Training for Musicians*.
Not for the faint-hearted! This book contains at least two years' study. But well worth the effort.

Louis Armstrong

Listening:
LOUIS ARMSTRONG, 'Basin Street Blues' from *Hot 5 and Hot 7*.
ELLA FITZGERALD, 'Rockin' in Rhythm' from *Sings the Duke Elling Songbook*.
CHET BAKER, 'But Not For Me' from *The Touch of Your Lips*.
AL JARREAU, 'Roof Garden' and 'Blue Rondo a la Turk' *Breakin' Away*.
BOBBY MCFERRIN, 'Walkin'' from *Spontaneous Inventions*.
The above recordings are all examples of scat-singing.

CHAPTER 12

The 'Clarinet' Register

The next register of the instrument, usually referred to as the 'Clarinet' register, is produced by adding the speaker key to fingering positions you have already learned. The notes thus obtained are a twelfth higher, i.e., an octave plus a perfect fifth. This can be confusing at first! The corresponding notes from the lower register are indicated by notes in parentheses.

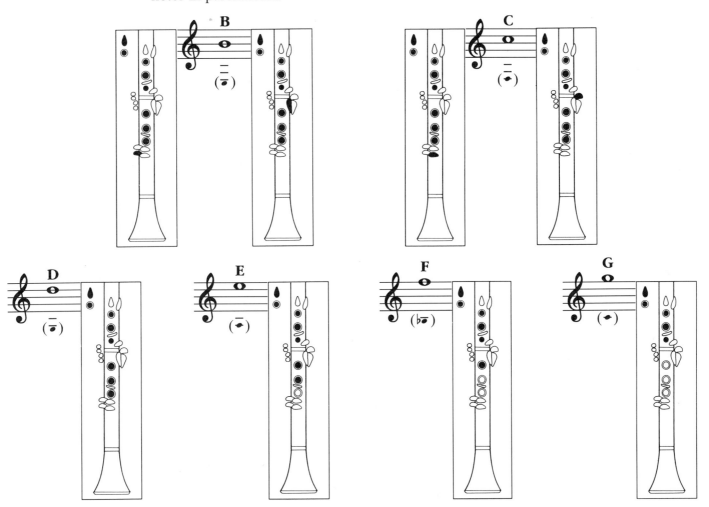

In the example below, the second of each pair of notes can be obtained simply by nudging the speaker key with the edge of the thumb. Be careful when doing this that you do not allow air to escape from the thumb hole—even tiny leaks can make the upper notes much more difficult to produce.

You will find it easier to produce these notes in tune and with a good tone if you observe the following points:

- Try to hear the upper note in your head before you actually play it, as with the exercise for singing intervals in the previous chapter.
- Keep the embouchure absolutely still, resisting the temptation to tighten as you move to the higher note.
- The throat should be open and relaxed—imagine an 'ah' shape.
- Maintain support for the air column by contracting the stomach muscles.

Make sure that in the first two examples you use both left- and right-hand fingerings for E/B and F/C.

Free tempo

Transposition

Here is 'P.M.', which you played in Chapter 2, written an octave higher in order to give you practice at reading these new notes. This process of moving a tune into a different register or key is known as **transposition**.

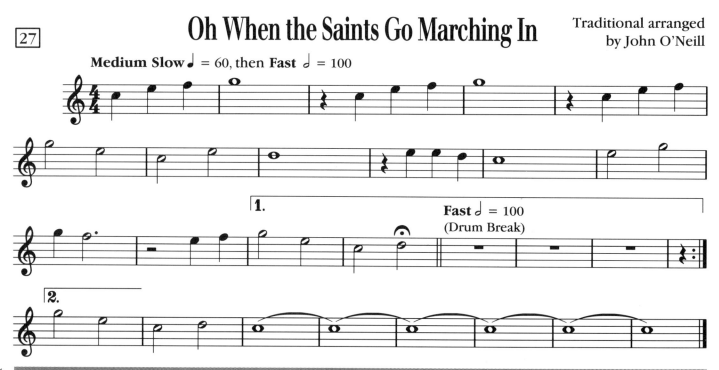

I have tried to reflect a New Orleans tradition in this arrangement of a jazz classic. At funerals there it is customary for marching bands which accompany the cortège to play slow, mournful music on the way to the cemetery and up-tempo, joyous tunes on the way back!

FURTHER STUDY

Writing/playing:

Write and/or play an octave higher the following tunes from earlier chapters: 'Blues for Beginners' [2], 'A la Mode' [3], 'Progression' [4], 'Out for the Count' [5], 'Third Attempt' [7] and 'South View' [8]. Remember to practise with both alternative fingerings where possible.

CHAPTER 13

The Break

One of the major technical problems of the clarinet is crossing the 'break', or moving to middle register B from the notes below. This involves considerable finger coordination and the exercise below will be a useful preparatory study.

- Do not be put off if the B sounds slightly muffled. Because of the number of pads that are being held down, it does have a denser tone quality than the A. The secret of getting the B to speak freely is to keep the embouchure still and the throat open and to support the breath by contracting the stomach muscles.
- The notes should be slurred throughout, with the exception of the initial attack note.
- For the purposes of the exercise you can keep the three right-hand fingers down while playing A. This will not drastically affect the pitch of the note and enables you to concentrate on the left hand, where the principal difficulty lies. Once you are able to play the exercise smoothly you will be ready to try moving the right-hand fingers as well.

Problems in achieving a smooth transition can usually be traced to one of the following faults:

- Air escaping from the tone-holes, and in particular from underneath the thumb and third fingers of either hand.
- Moving the embouchure.
- Failing to support the air column.
- Not keeping the throat open.
- A fault with the instrument, most commonly air leaking from under the C pad. With the left-hand B key depressed press gently on the C key with the right-hand first finger (see Fig. 23). If there is any 'play' the instrument is leaking.

Fig. 23
Checking for leaks under the C pad.

Do not be discouraged if you are not immediately successful at crossing the break. It is a technical challenge even for more advanced players.

'Breaking Point' and 'Transition' will provide similar technical practice with CD accompaniment.

Breaking Point

Transition

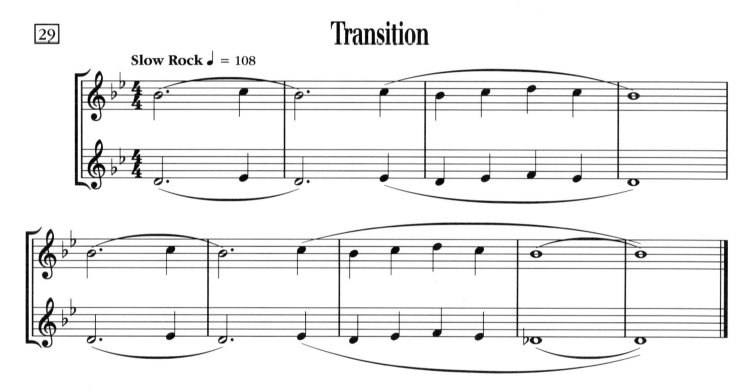

You may recognize the scale at the end of 'A Song For Sophie' as the same five-note scale which you improvised with at the end of 'Blue Jean' but transposed to begin on E instead of A. This is a pentatonic scale sometimes referred to as the 'minor pentatonic'.

A Song for Sophie

Scale and arpeggio practice: C major

You can practise improvising in C major using track [31] on the CD.

A minor

FURTHER STUDY

Playing:

Play an octave higher the following tunes from earlier chapters: 'Interstellar' [17], 'Home Bass' [9], 'Flat 5' [12], 'Blue Jean' [19], 'Bird Waltz' [24] and 'Devil Music' [25].

CHAPTER 14

Even Quavers

In classical music quavers, or eighth notes, are invariably given half the value of crotchets but in jazz they can be interpreted in different ways. This chapter will deal with the classical interpretation, sometimes referred to by jazz musicians as 'even quavers' or 'straight eighths'.

Single quavers are written thus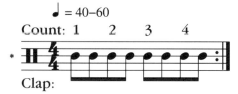

Beams

When there are two or more quavers
they may be connected by a beam, e.g. 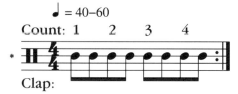 or

Perform the following exercises:

♩ = 40–60

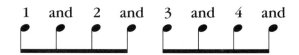

Quavers can also be counted in this way:

To perform the drumming exercise below sit on a chair with your feet on the floor and the palms of your hands resting on the top of your thighs. You should attempt it very slowly at first.

Right Hand

Left Hand

32

Like Benny

Medium Slow ♩ = 112

* This clef is used for percussion parts where pitch is unspecified.

'Tongue-twister' is an exercise for rapid tonguing, but do not strive for speed at the expense of even tone and rhythm. It is better to begin slowly and gradually increase the tempo, using a metronome if one is available.

Tongue-Twister

The next piece introduces two new notes—C♯/D♭ and A.

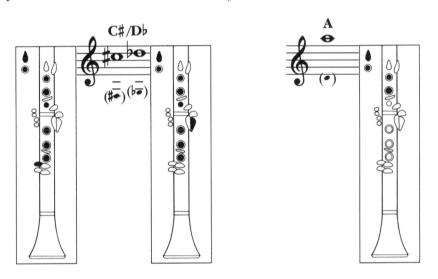

Jazz-Rock

'Lullaby' is an example of a tune in a jazz-rock style. This style always calls for an even-quaver interpretation.

If you experience problems with the tied rhythms, e.g. in bars 2 and 3, try playing the phrase first **without the tie**. This will help you to hear the correct placement of the notes.

D.C. al Fine

The direction *D.C. al Fine* is short for *Da Capo al Fine* (literally 'from the beginning to the end') and means repeat from the start of the piece and stop at the word *Fine*.

Rallentando

Rall. is an abbreviation of *rallentando*, meaning 'getting slower'.

Lullaby

Ted Gioia

Scale and arpeggio practice: G major

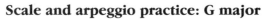

Practise improvising in G major using track 35 on the CD.

E minor

FURTHER STUDY

Listening:

TED GIOIA, 'Lullaby in G' from *The End of the Open Road.*

Playing:

Play the tune 'K.O.' 15 an octave higher.

Triplet Quavers

Triplet quavers occur when a crotchet beat is subdivided into three. They are notated like this:

Perform the following exercise:

One way of counting this rhythm is:

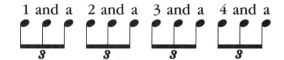

Drumming exercise

This exercise for rhythm and articulation would make an ideal daily warm-up, and should be practised on different notes throughout the clarinet range:

The pieces in this chapter introduce three new notes:

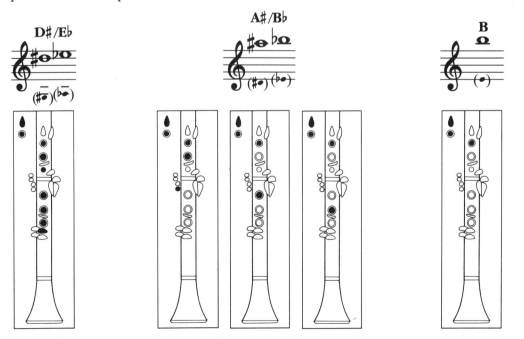

'Alicante' has a distinctly Spanish mood. Spanish music has inspired such famous musicians as Gil Evans, Miles Davis and Chick Corea.

36 ## Alicante

37 ## Exercise in Rhythm

Fine

D.S. al Fine
without repeat

Thelonious Monk

'The Loneliest Monk' is dedicated to the late Thelonious Monk, a pianist and composer whose extraordinary originality was coupled with a wry humour. Together with Charlie Parker, Dizzy Gillespie, Bud Powell, Kenny Clarke and Max Roach, he created the explosive style of music called Bebop which dominated jazz during the 1940s and the early 1950s.

The instruction *8va bassa ad lib.* means that the piece can also be played an octave lower if you wish.

38 **Slow Blues** ♩ = 86
8va bassa ad lib.

The Loneliest Monk

Scale practice: F major (2 octaves)

You can improvise in F major using track **20** on the CD.

D minor

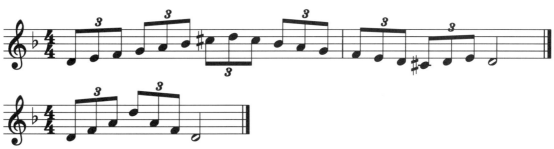

FURTHER STUDY

Listening:
MILES DAVIS with the GIL EVANS ORCHESTRA, *Sketches of Spain*.
MILES DAVIS SEXTET, 'Flamenco Sketches' from *Kind of Blue*.
CHICK COREA, 'Spain', 'Señor Mouse' and 'Armando's Rhumba' from *Chick Corea*.

Playing:
Play an octave higher 'Roberto' **21** and 'Apologies to Daisy' **26**.

CHAPTER 16

This chapter deals with quavers which are played with a 'swing' rather than with even interpretation.

Swing Quavers

It is important to understand that there is no **visual** distinction between swing (or 'jazz') quavers and even quavers. The notes are written the same way but interpreted differently, the on-beat quaver having a value of two thirds of a beat and the off-beat quaver one third of a beat. Swing quavers are therefore closely related to triplet quavers:

but to notate them as they are played would be untidy and unnecessarily complicated.

Practise the following exercise:

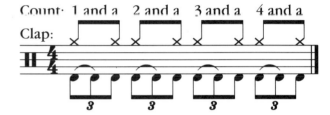

Scat-singing (see Chapter 11, p. 43) is an excellent way of establishing the correct 'feel' for jazz rhythms. One way of scatting jazz quavers is:

There are many other possibilities. Try inventing your own sounds. When the off-beat quaver is followed by silence, as in ''Trane Refrain' I prefer a more emphatic scat-sound:

To Swing Or Not To Swing?

You may be wondering how you are to know whether the quavers should be played 'straight' or 'swung'. In many cases this is indicated by the expression markings at the beginning of the piece. Sometimes the composer/arranger specifically requests the desired quaver interpretation. In other cases the idiom dictates what is required. For example, if the piece is marked 'jazz-rock', 'latin', 'bossa-nova' or 'calypso' the quavers are played even, but 'swing', or 'medium blues' indicates jazz quavers.* If in doubt, try both ways and make an artistic choice!

With jazz quavers a little extra emphasis is generally given to the off-beat quaver. To achieve this jazz musicians often slur from off-beat to on-beat. Tonguing all the on-beats can make the music sound laboured. In order to practise this kind of phrasing scales should be played as follows:

* At fast tempos, even in music in a swing idiom, the quavers are played straight, since a smooth swing interpretation is impossible to achieve.

You should also practise tonguing on every other off-beat quaver:

There are three new notes in this chapter, completing the 'clarinet' register:

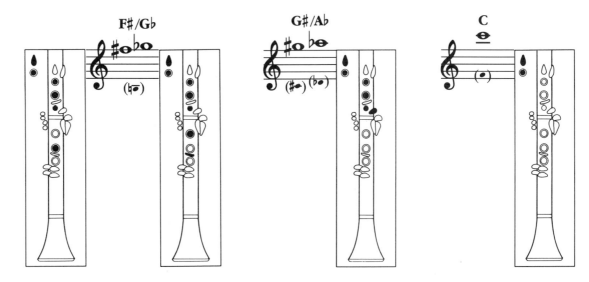

Round and Round Again

Jazz Waltz ♩ = 112 (Swing ♪s)

D.S. al Coda

CODA

John Coltrane

''Trane Refrain' is an example of the minor blues form which was often used by saxophonist John Coltrane (1926-1967), one of the most influential musicians in the history of jazz.

Anticipation

When an off-beat quaver is followed by a rest, as in the first six bars, or when it is tied over, as in the final six bars, it is often easier **not** to count the on-beat which immediately follows. This is because the off-beat quaver functions as an **anticipation** of the following beat. It can therefore feel rushed and uncomfortable to count the next beat, especially if the tempo is fast. Try to 'feel' this beat without consciously counting it.

'Trane Refrain

'Blue Monk' is one of Thelonious Monk's most celebrated compositions.

The Blues Scale/Passing Notes

In 'Blue Monk' there is a twelve-bar improvisation section. The suggested scale for improvisation is often referred to by jazz educators as the blues scale. It is similar to the minor pentatonic scales you used for 'Blue Jean' in Chapter 7 and 'Song for Sophie' in Chapter 13 but it has one extra note—the flattened fifth, which in this case is Gb. This note has a very strong blues feeling. It sounds extremely **dissonant** or restless when played by itself and is more often used by jazz musicians as a **passing note**, or connecting note, as in bars 1 and 3 of the upper part.

Blue Monk

Thelonious Monk

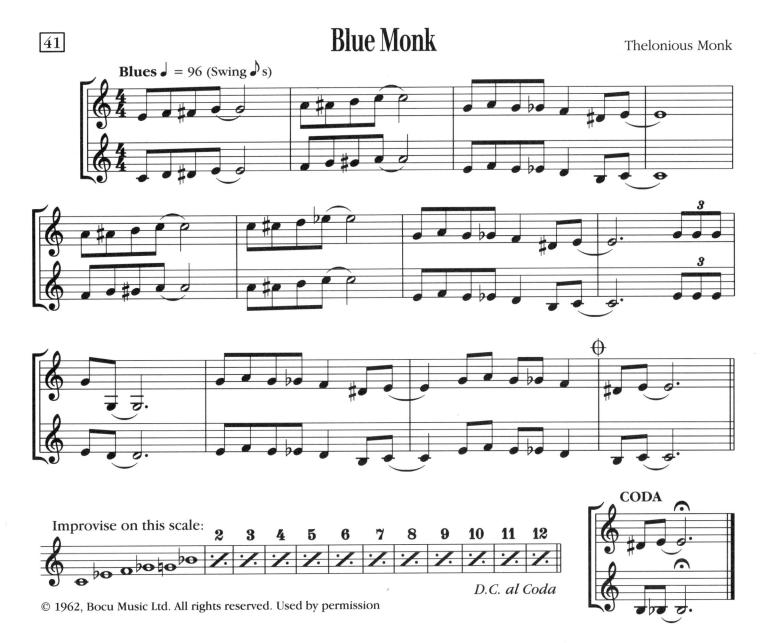

D.C. al Coda

Repetition

A key word to remember when improvising is **repetition**. Many beginner improvisers make the mistake of simply running up and down the scale rather aimlessly. Repetition of single notes in interesting rhythms is a good way of breaking this habit. Lester Young and Sonny Rollins provide masterly examples of how effective note repetition can be in a jazz solo. Equally important is the use of riffs (see Chapter 2, p. 21), for which you will find no better model than guitarist Charlie Christian. Experiment by inventing your own riffs on 'Blue Monk' using the given scale.

FURTHER STUDY

Listening:
JOHN COLTRANE, 'Mr P.C.' from *Giant Steps* as an example of a minor blues.
THELONIOUS MONK, 'Blue Monk' from *Greatest Hits* or *The Composer*.
CHARLIE CHRISTIAN, *The Genius of the Electric Guitar*.

Playing:
Play an octave higher 'James' 11 , 'Minor Problem' 13 , 'Sylvie's Dance' 14 , 'Times Remembered' 16 , and 'Romancing' 22 .

Construction of Major and Minor Scales

The illustration shows the distances between the component notes of the scale of C major, measured in tones and semitones. Semitones have already been discussed (see Chapter 4, p. 25). A tone is equal to two semitones. Do not be confused by the word tone. It has three possible meanings:

1. A means of expressing a particular distance between one note and another—as in the previous paragraph.
2. Sound, with special reference to quality, e.g. 'You have been trying to achieve a good **tone** on the saxophone'.
3. In American usage 'tone' is synonymous with the 'note', e.g. 'Play the first three **tones** of the C major scale'.

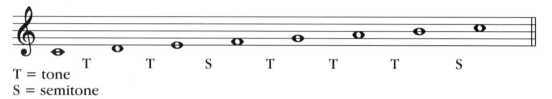

T = tone
S = semitone

Although the number of sharps or flats is different for every major scale the interrelationship of the notes is always the same. The sequence is always T T S T T T S.

For harmonic minor scales the sequence is as follows:

Notice the interval of a tone plus a semitone between the sixth and seventh degrees which gives the scale its exotic 'Middle Eastern' quality.

Interrelationship of Major and Minor Scales

The diagram opposite will help you to understand how the major and minor scales relate to one another.

It is called a cycle of fourths/fifths because the distance between each scale and the next one in the cycle is a perfect fifth if measured downwards and a perfect fourth if measured upwards.*

It is important to note the following points about the cycle:

1. The direction of movement is **clockwise**, following a fundamental tendency of chords to move by intervals of a fourth upwards or a fifth downwards.
2. It is a cycle of increasing 'flatness' or decreasing 'sharpness', proceeding from one to seven flats, and from seven to one sharps.
3. Each major scale contains only one altered note in comparison with the previous scale in the cycle. This is the fourth note of the new scale, which is flattened by one semitone. For example, the only difference between C and F major is the B♭.
4. Sharps and flats cannot be mixed in the key signature.
5. Each harmonic minor scale starts on the sixth degree of its relative major and contains the same notes except for the seventh note which is raised by one semitone. The seventh note of both major and minor scales is often referred to as the **leading note** because of its tendency to lead back to the key note.

* For more information on intervals see the section on 'Ear Training', p. 40

Cycle of 4ths/5ths

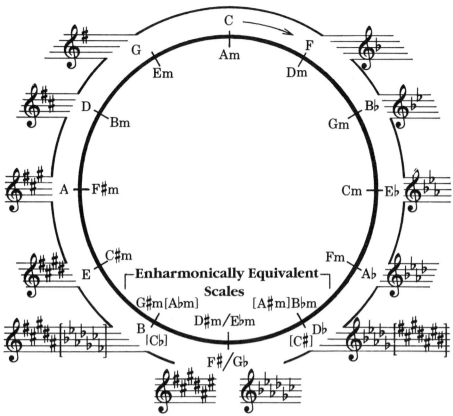

Enharmonic Scales

Notice the three enharmonic scales. Each of these scales can be thought of in two different ways (see Chapter 8, p. 32). The example below illustrates this. The scales are written differently but sound the same.

Practising the Scales

You should start with C major and A minor scales and arpeggios and proceed through the cycle.

You should practise the scales over the entire range and not simply from keynote to keynote. Start on the lowest available key-note, play up to the highest note in that scale which you are able to play, down to the lowest note which you can play and then back up to finish where you started. The example below shows how this would apply to the B♭ major scale and arpeggio.

Scale Variations

I would suggest practising each scale with its arpeggio and relative minor scale and arpeggio for at least a week. Once you have mastered the basic scale you should start to practise variations. Below are just two examples in the key of C major:

You should also experiment with many different rhythms and articulations. The possibilities are endless. The complaint that scales are boring only comes from the unimaginative! If you want to learn to improvise you must learn to be creative in your practice.

FURTHER STUDY

Playing:

In order to make your practice of major and minor scales and arpeggios more interesting and enjoyable I strongly recommend that you purchase Volume 24 of Jamey Aebersold's play-along series, entitled 'Major and Minor', which contains backing tracks for all keys. However, please be aware that Jamey uses a different form of the minor scale—the Dorian minor. Appendix 2 contains further details about this series of play-alongs.

CHAPTER 18

Off-Beat Phrases

So far all the phrases which you have played have started on the beat. The pieces in this chapter feature phrases which begin **off** the beat.

To begin with you may find it helpful to indicate the position of every quaver by counting as follows:

When you play phrases which begin off the beat you will therefore be entering on the 'and'. The example below shows how this counting method could be applied to the first two bars of 'A Bossa for Betty'.

Eventually you will probably be able to dispense with counting the 'and'.
The symbol ⁊ is a quaver rest, worth half a beat. The note which follows it in the second bar is a dotted crotchet, worth one and a half beats. The off-beat dotted crotchet can therefore also be written:

A Bossa for Betty

'Sister Caroline' features off-beat entries in a jazz-quaver context. Remember that an on-beat quaver rest is worth two thirds of a beat! The off-beat quaver is therefore later than when you are playing with an even-quaver interpretation. In order to achieve the correct interpretation listen to the CD and then try scatting what the clarinet is playing using the syllables written between the staves.

Sister Caroline

So far you have improvised using different scales. The next piece gives you the opportunity to improvise with a sequence of three arpeggios—C, F and G major, indicated by the symbols C, F and G. Play just the arpeggio notes to begin with. In other words in the first bar you can play either C, E or G, in the second bar F, A or C and in the third bar G, B or D. This sounds simple enough but you will discover that it is quite a challenge to keep track of where you are in the sequence. If you find that you keep losing your place try playing just the lowest note of each arpeggio until you begin to feel the rhythm in which the chords are moving.

Triad Exercise

CHAPTER

19

The Dotted Crotchet Followed by a Quaver

The new rhythm that you will meet in this chapter is the dotted crotchet followed by a quaver. The exercises below will help you to understand how this rhythm relates to previous rhythms you have learnt. They should be performed using both even- and jazz-quaver interpretations. It is particularly important that you count the beat immediately preceding the off-beat quaver.

N.B. (b) and (c), and (e) and (f) are identical rhythmically but notated differently.

Lucky Rhythm

Tony Crowle

D.S. al Fine

Summer Hummer

Bossa Nova ♩ = 138 (Even ♪s)

Modes

The improvised solo at the end of 'I Will Call You' uses the Phrygian **mode**. A mode is another name for a scale. Using the notes of each major scale it is possible to create six additional scales or modes using each different degree of the scale as a tonal centre. Playing the F major scale starting on the third degree produces A Phrygian. This mode is highly evocative of Spanish music.

I Will Call You

♩ = 124 (Even ♪s)

D.C. al Coda

CODA

Improvise using this scale (A Phrygian):

fade out

FURTHER STUDY

Listening:

MILES DAVIS, 'Flamenco Sketches' from *Kind of Blue*, one of the first recordings to explore modal improvisation. This is perhaps the most famous example of the use of the Phrygian mode in jazz.

Playing/Singing:

Listen to 'So What' from MILES DAVIS' *Kind of Blue*. The rhythm of the answering phrase played by the saxophones and trumpet in response to the bass figure is a dotted crotchet followed by a quaver. Try first singing and then playing this phrase along with the record.

CHAPTER 20

On-Beat Quaver Followed by Two Off-Beats

Another extremely common rhythm in jazz is the on-beat quaver followed by two consecutive off-beats. This may be encountered in various 'disguises' as will be apparent from the following exercises.

N.B. When clapped (b), (c), (d) and (e) sound the same, since the difference between them is only the *duration* of the notes and not their rhythmic position.

The instruction *8va ad lib.* at the beginning of 'Country Road' means that this piece may also be played an octave higher.

Country Road

48

Lazy Swing ♩ = 72 (Lazy Swing ♪ s)

'Euphrates' uses the modes of E Dorian (scale of D major starting on E) and F Dorian (scale of E♭ major starting on F). This scale may be thought of as a variation of the minor scale since the first five notes are identical with those of the harmonic minor. It is the most commonly used mode in jazz.

This composition also introduces the **ascending melodic minor** scale. This is another variation of the minor scale in which the sixth note is raised by one semitone. Another way of thinking of it is as a major scale with the third note lowered one semitone.*

It is quite possible that you may get lost in your improvisation to begin with. If this happens try the following sequence of exercises:

1. Play the CD and count carefully through each eight-bar section.
2. Play a solo in semibreves only—one note to each bar. This will give you time to count the bars.
3. Play a solo using only minims.
4. Play a solo using only crotchets.

Practising in this way will help you develop your 'internal clock' which measures the passing of time in music. Eventually you will be able to 'feel' a two-, four-, or eight-bar phrase without actually counting it.

* Classical musicians use a different form of the melodic scale in which the sixth and seventh notes are lowered by a semitone as it descends, i.e:

Jazz musicians prefer to use the notes of the ascending form whether the scale is played rising or falling, hence the name by which it is known.

Euphrates

Don Rendell

'Endless Night' is an example of the tango, a passionate Argentinian dance form. Like other South American dances it requires an even-quaver interpretation.

Endless Night

Tango ♩ = 120 (Even ♪s)

FURTHER STUDY

Listening:

Miles Davis, 'So What' from *Kind of Blue*. This is a celebrated example of the use of the Dorian mode in jazz.

CHAPTER 21

Consecutive Off-Beats

You are already familiar with rhythms which involve two consecutive off-beats (Chapter 20, p. 65), but it is not uncommon to find a whole string of them. When playing even quavers consecutive off-beats can be counted as follows:

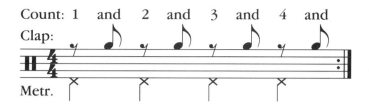

With jazz quavers counting becomes more problematic. At slow tempos you could adopt the following approach:

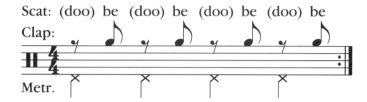

However, at faster tempos there is no space to count the on-beat (see Chapter 16: Anticipation, p. 56) and you will have to rely on developing the correct 'feel'.

Perform the previous exercise setting the metronome at about 80 beats per minute and gradually increasing the tempo to 160.

You will probably notice one of two tendencies as the tempo increases: either the off-beat quaver becomes even rather than swung, which is a sign of rushing or playing ahead of the beat, or the off-beat gets closer and closer to the following beat, which is symptomatic of playing late or behind the beat. You will also notice a point where to say the 'doo' begins to feel uncomfortable and rushed; so dispense with vocalizing the on-beat and try to feel the rhythm.

'My Little Suede Shoes' is one of Charlie Parker's most famous compositions and one of the earliest examples of the calypso rhythm in jazz. The calypso is a dance form which originated in Trinidad. It is characterized by a strong 'two-in-the-bar' feeling, which is achieved by the bass playing mainly on the first and third beats of each bar.

Charlie Parker

My Little Suede Shoes

Charlie Parker

51

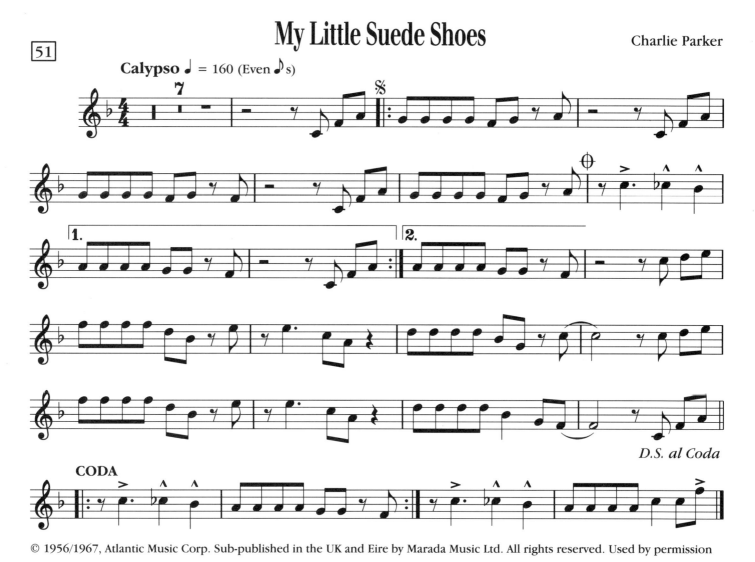

'Doxy' was written by Sonny Rollins (b. 1929), who established himself in the band led by drummer Max Roach and trumpeter Clifford Brown and whose unmistakable tone, and unique sense of phrasing and rhythm make him one of the greatest jazz soloists.

Doxy

Sonny Rollins

52

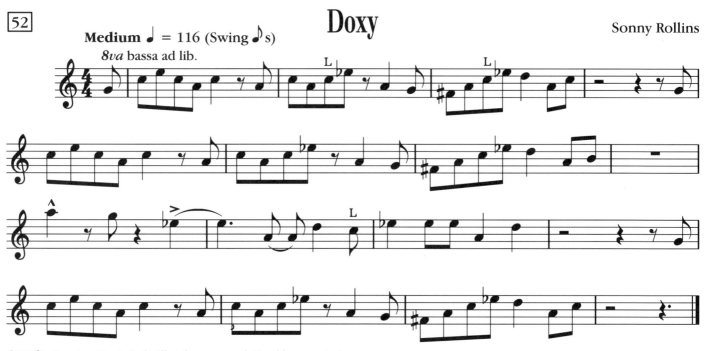

The Right Time

Dave Cliff

Minor Blues ♩ = 120 (Swing ♪s)

'Happy Man' was written by Jimmy Giuffre (b. 1921), one of the great original voices of jazz, whose career has spanned six decades. A multi-instrumentalist with a unique, breathy clarinet sound, composer/arranger and bandleader, he is perhaps best known for the trios which he has led featuring outstanding musicians like bassist Red Mitchell, guitarist Jim Hall, valve trombonist Bob Brookmeyer, pianist Paul Bley and bassist Steve Swallow.

For this piece he suggests: 'Avoid letting the eighth notes fall into a constant pattern; one approach would be to drag or delay the tempo and then catch up.'

Jimmy Giuffre

Happy Man

Jimmy Giuffre

Medium Blues ♩ = 132 (Swing ♪s)

FURTHER STUDY

Listening:

CHARLIE PARKER, 'My Little Suede Shoes' from *Charlie Parker*.
SONNY ROLLINS, 'Doxy' from *Prestige Years Vol. 2*.
DAVE CLIFF, 'The Right Time' from *The Right Time*.
JIMMY GIUFFRE, 'Happy Man' from *Seven Pieces*.

CHAPTER 22

Triplet Crotchets

Triplet crotchets are exactly twice the length of triplet quavers and therefore involve grouping three notes against two beats. The following clapping exercise will help you to understand the relationship between triplet quavers and triplet crotchets:

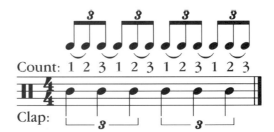

Once you have mastered the above try this exercise for tapping triplet crotchets against regular crotchets:

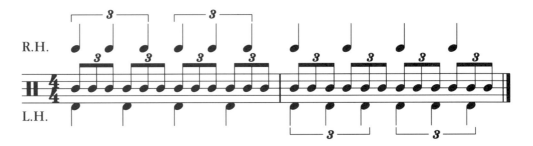

The triplet quavers have been written to enable you to work out the rhythm mathematically but you should aim at being able to count the crotchet pulse and 'feel' the triplet crotchet rhythm.

Triplet crotchets should be played absolutely evenly—a common fault is to play the second one early and the third one late so that the rhythm resembles ♪ ♩ ♪ rather than ♩ ♩ ♩.

The final section of 'Tango Cool' will give you a good opportunity to differentiate these two rhythms.

55 ## Tango Cool

Ted Gioia

56 ## Frankincense

Don Rendell

'Peace' was written by Horace Silver (b. 1928), who first received public acclaim as a member of Miles Davis' rhythm section of the early 1950s and later became famous as a composer and bandleader in his own right.

Peace

Horace Silver

FURTHER STUDY

Listening:
TED GIOIA/MARK LEWIS, 'Tango Cool' from *Tango Cool*.
HORACE SILVER, 'Peace' from *Blowin' the Blues Away*.

Horace Silver

CHAPTER 23

Harmony

Up until now your attempts at improvisation have been confined to different scales or modes. In order to become a complete musician you will also have to study **harmony**. Harmony is concerned with *simultaneous* sounds. It is one of the three great building blocks of music—the others being **rhythm**, or the organisation of notes in time, and **melody**, which deals with the ordering of *successive* sounds. It is not the intention of this book to deal with harmony in depth but rather to whet your appetite.

In Chapter 8 you were introduced to the idea of a triad. You can form a triad by taking any note of any major or minor scale and adding diatonic notes at intervals of a third. (Diatonic notes are those which belong to the scale in question.) Observe that the notes will either all be written on lines or all on spaces:

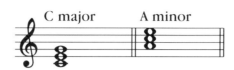

This procedure of building chords by stacking up notes in thirds can be extended to as many as seven notes, in which case all the notes in the scale are being played simultaneously. The example below shows a rearrangement of the notes of the C major scale.

If you have access to a piano and rudimentary knowledge of the keyboard you will benefit by exploring some of these exotic possibilities. If not, you should consider taking up the keyboard as a second study. Many jazz musicians have found that knowledge of the keyboard opens up exciting new possibilities in improvisation. Dizzy Gillespie, Bob Brookmeyer and Gerry Mulligan are just three famous examples.

Diatonic Chords

In modern jazz the four-note chord (with added seventh) is the basic unit of harmony. It is therefore important for you to get to know the diatonic four-note chords in each major and harmonic minor scale. Below are examples for the keys of C major and A minor.

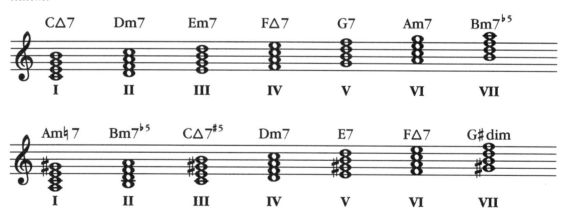

Chord Symbols

Below each chord is a Roman numeral which identifies the scale degree on which it is based. Written above each chord is a **chord symbol**, which is a kind of harmonic shorthand used by jazz musicians to identify different chord types. You need not know all of these at present. The following are the most important:

$\triangle 7$ = major seventh (major triad + major seventh measured from lowest note)
7 = seventh (major triad + minor seventh)
m7 = minor seventh (minor triad + minor seventh)
m7$^{\flat 5}$ = minor seventh with a flattened fifth. This chord is indicated by some jazz educators with the symbol Ø.

The following tune will serve as a model in this exploration of jazz harmony.

Fall '90

Below is the chord progression to 'Fall '90'.

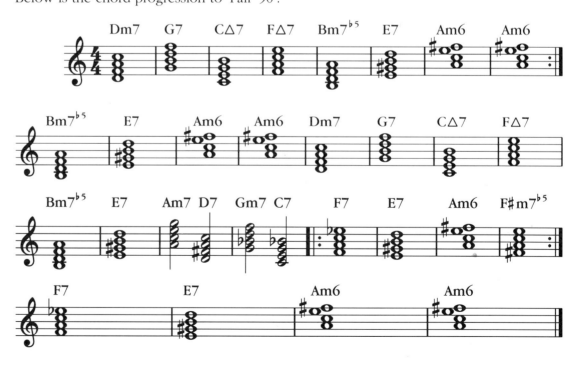

If you look at the direction of movement or **resolution** of the chords you will see that much of the time it follows the direction of the cycle of fourths/fifths (p. 59)

II-V-I Progression

The harmony of this tune largely consists of movement from the II chord to the V chord to the I chord in the keys of C major and A minor.* This is the **II-V-I progression**, by far the most common chord progression in jazz.

The following sequence of exercises will help to familiarize you with the chord progression of 'Fall '90'. It may take you a long time to master them, but please persevere—the knowledge you gain will sharpen your ear and help your improvisation to become more sophisticated. A similar sequence of exercises could be used for learning the harmony of any standard tune.

N.B. Chords are written for reference only. All these exercises should be memorized and played by ear.

- Sing and then play the **root** progression. The root is the scale degree on which the chord is built. There are different ways of performing this exercise, since you have a choice of whether you move up or down to the next note, e.g.:

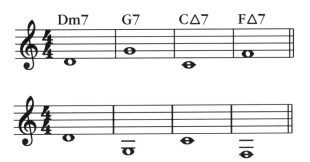

- Sing and play the chord progression, one note to each beat, e.g.:

N.B. For the bars with two chords you should play just the root and the third, e.g.:

The arpeggios can also be played descending, e.g.:

As a further variation, the arpeggio shapes could be transposed to different registers of the instrument. This principle could also be applied to the exercises which follow.

* The Am6 chord (A-C-E-F♯) has been substituted for the Am♮7 but its harmonic function is the same.

● Improvise a melodic line in semibreves, using chord notes only. This is an excellent exercise for **voice-leading**, or the smooth connection of one chord with another. It is usually better to move from one chord to the next by moving in small steps, although bigger intervals can be used for dramatic effect. Feel free to repeat notes if they are common to both chords, e.g.:

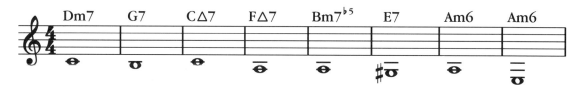

● Improvise a line in minims, using chord notes only, e.g.:

● Improvise in crotchets using chord notes only. This is closely related to the 'walking bass' technique used by jazz bass-players. You may need to make room for breathing spaces, by leaving out notes here and there, e.g.:

● Improvise in free rhythm using chord notes only, e.g.:

● Improvise freely using additional notes from the C major and A minor scales and any others which sound good!

FURTHER STUDY

Playing:

JERRY COKER, *Jerry Coker's Jazz Keyboard*. An excellent book for developing jazz keyboard skills, for pianists and non-pianists.

LIONEL GRIGSON, *Practical Jazz*. A thorough exploration of jazz harmony and its relevance for improvisation.

CHAPTER 24

The 'Altissimo' Register

It is difficult to define the upper limit of the 'altissimo' register, which begins with C♯ on the second leger line above the stave. Most fingering charts will go to G above this, but it is possible to extend the range further, at least as far as E♭ above this G. However, mastery of the altissimo register is an advanced technique, and, since this book is aimed at the beginner to intermediate player, I have decided to set the limit at F, which is a relatively comfortable note to produce. Those players interested in exploring further should consult the references for additional reading at the end of this chapter.

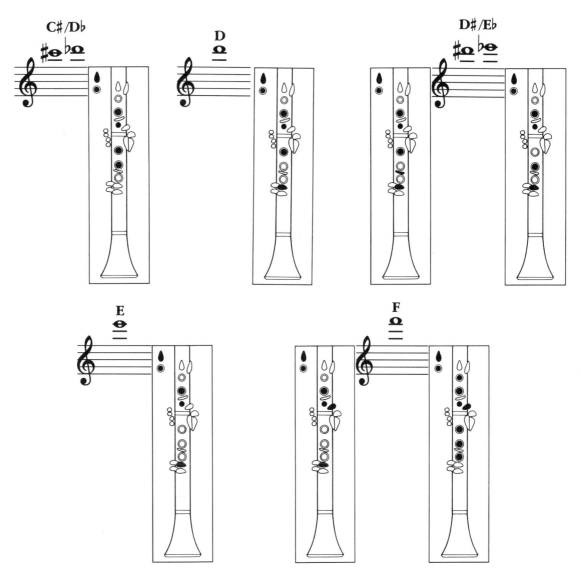

The fingering exercises below have been designed to help you overcome the technical difficulties which the altissimo register presents. Please observe the following points when practising them:

- Make sure you are supporting the air column by contracting the stomach muscles, otherwise your sound will tend to be thin and your intonation flat.
- The throat should be open and relaxed—imagine the vowel sound 'ee'. This will help you to produce a fuller tone.
- Keep the mouth corners pulling slightly up and back towards the corners of the eyes.
- A reed that is too soft will make it difficult to play these notes in tune, so if you feel you are observing the above points and still playing flat it may be worth putting on a new reed or trying a reed which is slightly harder.
- On many B♭ clarinets the use of the right hand little finger on the A♭/E♭ key improves intonation on the notes D and above. On other instruments this may not be necessary. You will need to experiment to find out what is right for your clarinet.
- In order to master the rather awkward fingering positions you should first slur the exercises. However, articulation is also particularly difficult in this register so you should practise tonguing the exercises as well, trying to ensure that the sound of the tongue touching the reed does not disturb the purity of the tone.
- Use both alternative fingerings for D♯/E♭ wherever possible.

♩ = 50–100 or faster

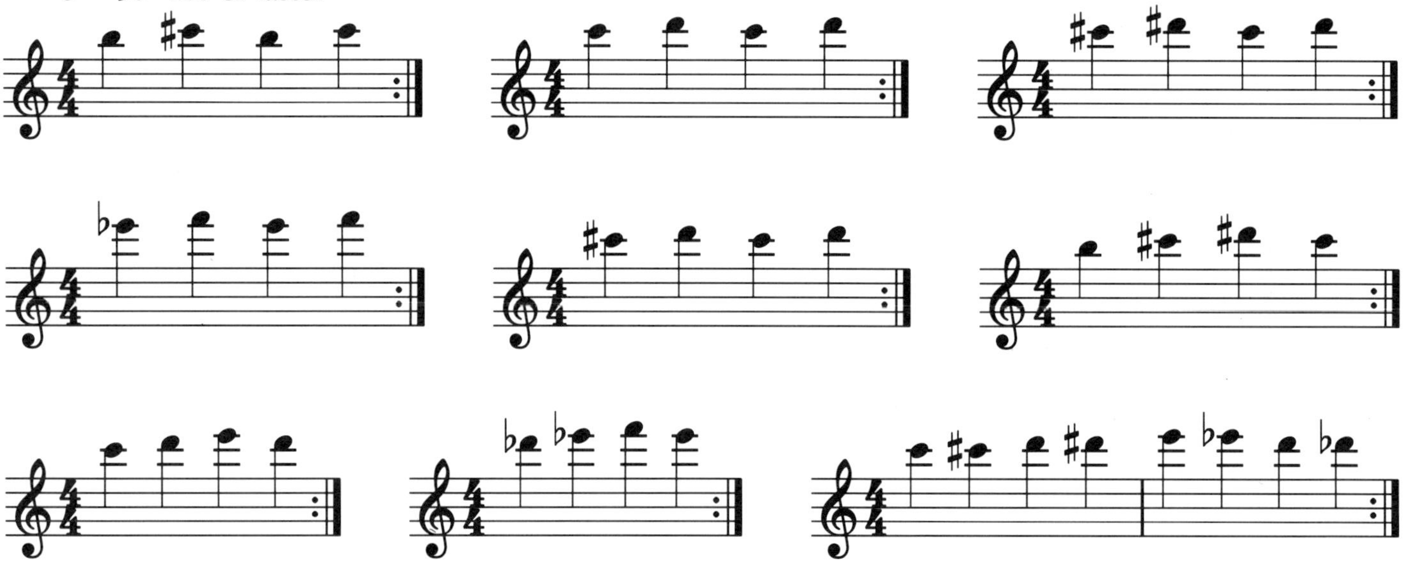

59

Familiarity

Pete Hurt

Ballad ♩ = 58 (Even ♪s)

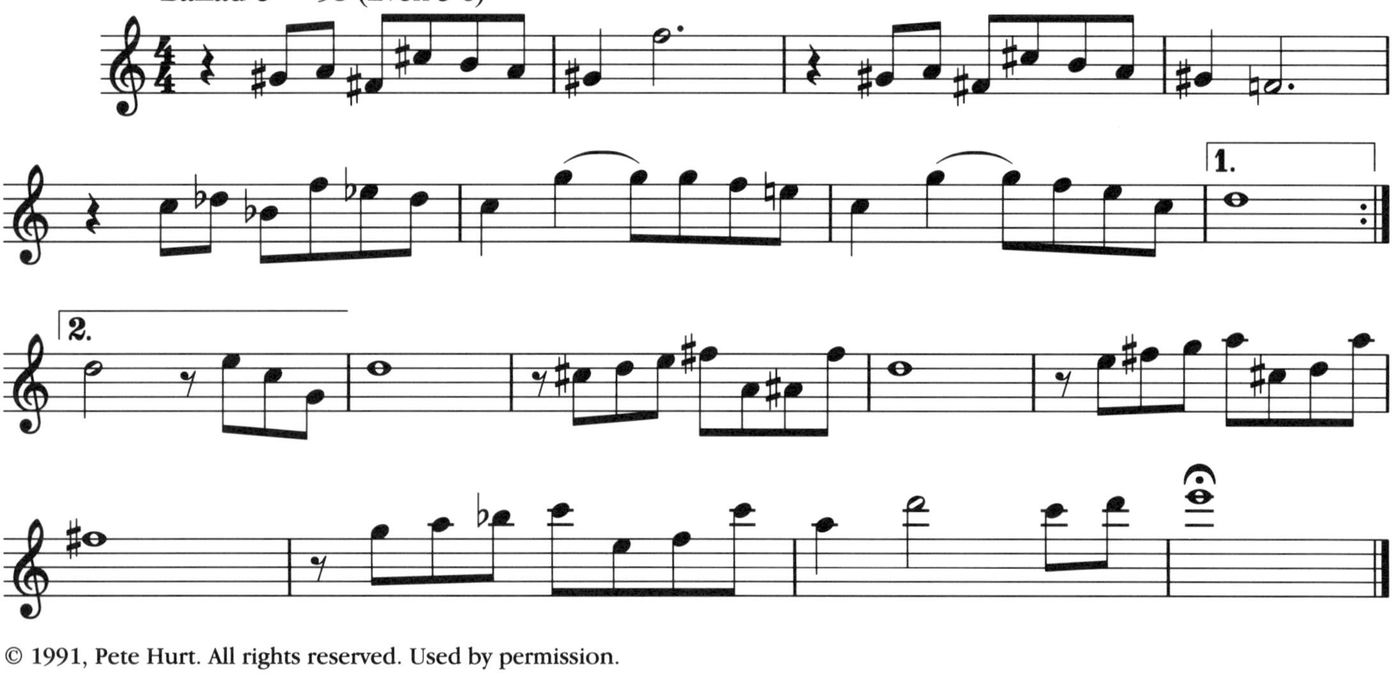

Here is a beautiful melody from the vast treasury of Irish folk music. It has been recorded by the pop-singer Van Morrison, whose music is heavily influenced by jazz and blues.

She Moved Through the Fair

Traditional arranged
by John O'Neill

FURTHER STUDY

Playing:

For additional practice in the altissimo register transpose the following tunes from earlier chapters:

Up two octaves: 'Blues for Beginners' ☐2☐, 'A la Mode' ☐3☐, 'Progression' ☐4☐, 'Out for the Count' ☐5☐, 'P.M.' ☐6☐, 'Third Attempt' ☐7☐, 'South View' ☐8☐, 'Home Bass' ☐9☐, 'Los Azules' ☐10☐, 'Flat 5' ☐12☐, 'Roberto' ☐21☐, 'Devil Music' ☐25☐, 'Apologies to Daisy' ☐26☐.

Up one octave: 'Transition' ☐29☐, ''Trane Refrain' ☐40☐, 'Blue Monk' ☐41☐.

Reading:

JACK BRYMER, *Clarinet*. The section Fingering Corrections in Chapter 3 is particularly useful for those wishing to explore further the altissimo register.

CHAPTER

25

Semiquavers and Semiquaver Rests

Semiquavers, or sixteenth notes, are half the length of even quavers. Rhythms which involve semiquavers can look very complicated—suddenly the manuscript becomes very black!—but try not to be intimidated. If you look carefully at the rhythm exercises on p. 82 you will see that the mathematical relationship between the notes in the semiquaver examples in 2/4 is the same as in the quaver examples 4/4 which are written next to them. It is only the unit of time that you are counting which changes.

For this reason you may initially find it helpful to count the quaver beat when playing semiquaver rhythms. This means that the first example would be counted as follows:

Another option would be to count like this:

You could apply the same principle to the other exercises, but work towards being able to count crotchet beats.

The sign 𝄿 is a semiquaver rest.

Drumming Exercise

The following exercise will provide excellent practice both for rhythm and articulation. It should be played for a few minutes at each practice session as part of your warm-up until you have mastered it. Play it on various notes throughout the range.

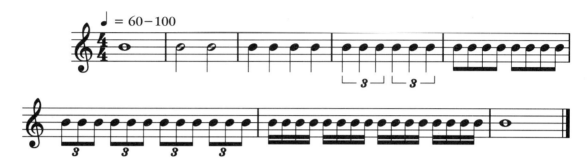

Spanish Steps

61

Persuasion

62

Roland Perrin

Grace Notes

The F♯ written before the G in bars 12 and 15 of 'It's All Yours' is a **grace note**. It should be played on the beat and 'crushed' against the note which follows. Try to imitate the example on the CD.

It's All Yours

'Early Bird' was written by Adrian Litvinoff, a bassist and composer who works with the sextet Footprints and in a big band specializing in the music of Don Ellis. He is energetic in promoting the use of improvised music in schools and colleges, most notably in partnership with the Grand Union Orchestra.

The solo section is based on the Mixolydian mode, which is formed from the fifth degree of any major scale. F Mixolydian is therefore related to B♭ major. Feel free to use notes from outside the scale as passing notes.

64

Early Bird

Adrian Litvinoff

CHAPTER

26

Since the early 1960s there has been increasing experimentation with time signatures other than 3/4 or 4/4 in jazz. Pianist Dave Brubeck, alto saxophonist Paul Desmond and trumpeter Don Ellis were among the first to experiment widely with unusual time signatures.

6/8 Time

6/8 time means that you count six quavers to a bar, although at faster tempos this is nearly always counted in two (dotted-crotchet beats), with each beat subdivided into three. The exercises below show both possibilities for counting.

Dave Brubeck Quartet

5/4 Time

Like many of the more complex time signatures, such as 7/4 or 11/4, 5/4 is nearly always subdivided into a combination of two- and three-beat groupings. You will probably find it easier to count these groups of two or three rather than the actual number of beats in the bar. In 'Five Jive' the subdivision is three followed by two.

Irregular Phrasing

Irregular phrasing occurs when a phrase is repeated in unpredictable positions within the bar. In 'Straight, No Chaser' the phrasing is completely asymmetrical, making it very difficult to know where the 'one' is. Careful counting is the only solution.

'Lady Pres' is a pastiche of the style of Lester Young, famous principally as a tenor saxophonist but also a fine clarinettist, nicknamed 'Pres', short for President, by singer Billie Holiday, because he was her favourite player. The title derives from his habit of calling everyone 'Lady' irrespective of whether they were male or female! This is how Billie Holiday came to be called Lady Day. Phrasing across the bar-line and suggesting different metric subdivisions, most commonly 3/4 against 4/4, were characteristic of his improvisational technique, and I have tried to reflect this in 'Lady Pres'.

Lester Young

Lady Pres

Medium-Up ♩ = 144 (Swing ♪s)

FURTHER STUDY

Listening:

CHARLES MINGUS, 'Better Git It In Your Soul' from *Mingus Ah Um*. Another example of 6/8 time.

DAVE BRUBECK, *Time Out*. Features Paul Desmond's composition 'Take Five', one of the most famous tunes in an unusual time signature.

LESTER YOUNG, 'Lady Be Good' and 'I Ain't Got Nobody' from *The Essential Count Basie Vol. 1*.

Playing:

LOESBERG, JOHN, ed., *An Irish Tunebook*. Parts One and Two. The books contain much immensely enjoyable and exciting music in 6/8 time. They also provide excellent practice for technique, rhythm and articulation and good source material for learning by heart and transposition.

Reading:

LEWIS PORTER, *Lester Young*.

Part Three: Appendices

BIBLIOGRAPHY

The following publications are those to which specific reference is made in the sections entitled Further Study.

BERENDT, JOACHIM E. *The Jazz Book* (London, Paladin, 1984). Useful both as a reference book and as an introduction to the subject.

BRYMER, JACK. *Clarinet* in the series 'Yehudi Menuhin Music Guides' (London, Macdonald and Janes, 1976)

COKER, JERRY. *Jerry Coker's Jazz Keyboard* (Florida, Columbia Pictures Publications, 1984)

GIDDINS, GARY. *Celebrating Bird: The Triumph of Charlie Parker* (New York, Beech Tree Books, William Morrow and Company, Inc., 1987)

GRIGSON, LIONEL. *Practical Jazz* (London, Stainer and Bell, 1988)

HINDEMITH, PAUL. *Elementary Training for Musicians* (London, Schott, 1946)

KERNFELD, BARRY, ed. *The New Grove Dictionary of Jazz* (London, Macmillan Press, 1988). A significant investment but worth every penny. The most complete and authoritative reference work on the subject.

PORTER, LEWIS. *Lester Young* (London, Macmillan Press, 1985)

REISNER, ROBERT. *Bird: The Legend of Charlie Parker* (New York, Citadel Press, 1962)

RUSSELL, ROSS. *Bird Lives* (New York, Charterhouse, 1973)

SADIE, STANLEY, ed. *The New Grove Dictionary of Music and Musicians* (London, Macmillan, 1980)

These books are recommended for general background and interest:

GIOIA, TED. *The Imperfect Art* (New York, Oxford University Press, 1988). A unique and thought-provoking discussion on the place of jazz in modern culture.

GRIME, KITTY. *Jazz at Ronnie Scott's* (London, Robert Hale, 1979). A fascinating collection of anecdotes and aphorisms by musicians who have played at the club.

HENTOFF, NAT and SHAPIRO, NAT. *Hear Me Talkin' to Ya: the Story of Jazz by the Men Who Made It* (New York, Rinehart, 1955). Complements perfectly the Kitty Grime book noted above.

The books below are recommended as supplementary or additional material:

BACH, J.S. trans. GIAMPIERI. *21 Pezzi per Clarinetto* (Milan, Ricordi, 1959). Transcribed from the works for solo violin and cello, these studies are masterpieces of melodic invention. Intermediate to advanced.

GIUFFRE, JIMMY. *Jazz Phrasing and Interpretation* (New York, Associated Music Publishers, 1969). A thorough exploration of this subject by one of the great voices of the jazz clarinet and a respected teacher.

GERSHWIN, GEORGE, arr. DE SMET. *The Music of George Gershwin for Clarinet* (London, Wise Publications, 1987). Beautiful melodies, of beginner to intermediate standard, suitable for reading or learning by heart.

KERN, JEROME, arr. DE SMET. *The Music of Jerome Kern for Clarinet* (London, Wise Publications, 1990). Of similar value to the Gershwin book noted above.

RAE, JAMES. *40 Modern Studies for Solo Clarinet* (London, Universal Edition, 1991). These studies are valuable for developing technique and reading skills. Beginner to advanced standard.

SHANAPHY, ED, and ISACOFF, STUART. *Dick Hyman's Professional Chord Changes and Substitutions For 100 Tunes Every Musician Should Know* (New York, Ekay Music, 1986). Valuable for building a repertoire of tunes. The melodies and chords are accurate and there is the added bonus of lyrics, which are indispensable for learning how to phrase a tune properly.

DISCOGRAPHY

Every effort has been made to ensure that this discography is as up to date and accurate as possible at the time of writing, but since recordings are being deleted and reissued all the time it is impossible to guarantee that all are currently available. Similarly, if a recording is not listed in the format you require, e.g. CD, record or cassette, you should not conclude that it is permanently unavailable in that format.

Should you find it difficult to obtain any of the recordings, try looking in one of the many specialist jazz record shops, most of which have second-hand sections and also import recordings from other countries.

This discography was compiled with the expert assistance of Bob Glass of Ray's Jazz Shop Ltd, 180 Shaftesbury Avenue, London.

Key: CD = compact disc; LP = long-playing record; C = cassette

ARMSTRONG, LOUIS. *Hot 5 and Hot 7 (1925–1928)* (Giants of Jazz GOJCD 0242). These recordings feature Johnny Dodds, one of the leading clarinettists in the New Orleans style.

BAKER, CHET. *The Touch of Your Lips* (Steeplechase SCS-1122 [LP])

BASIE, COUNT. *Swinging the Blues* (That's Jazz TJCD 0004 [CD], TJMC 0004 [C, LP]). These are reissues of the Decca recordings.

—*The Essential Count Basie Vol. 1* (CBS 460061 1 [LP], 460061 2 [CD] 460061 4 [C])

—*The Essential Count Basie Vol. 2* (CBS 460828 1 [LP], 460828 2 [CD], 460828 4 [C])

BECHET, SIDNEY. *The Legendary Sidney Bechet* (RCA Bluebird NL 86590 [LP], NK 86590 [C], ND 86590 [CD])

BRUBECK, DAVE. *Time Out* (CBS [Sony Music] 4606111 [LP], 4606112 [CD], 4604114 [C])

CHRISTIAN, CHARLIE. *The Genius of the Electric Guitar* from the CBS Jazz Masterpieces series (CBS [Sony Music] 4606122 [CD], 4606121 [LP], 4606124 [C]). Features Benny Goodman on clarinet.

CLIFF, DAVE. *The Right Time* (Miles Music MM074 [LP])

COLTRANE, JOHN. *Giant Steps* (Atlantic 7567 81337 2 [CD], ATL 50239 [LP])

—*A Love Supreme* (Impulse MCA DMCL 1648 [CD], MCL 1648 [LP] MCLC 1648 [C])

COREA, CHICK. *Chick Corea* from the Compact Jazz and Walkman Jazz series (Polydor [Polygram] 8313652 [CD], 8313654 [C])

DANIELS, EDDIE. *Nepenthe* (GRP 96072 [CD])

DAVERN, KENNY. *One Hour Tonight* (Musicmasters MMD 20148A [LP], CIJD 401482 [C])

DAVIS, MILES. *Kind of Blue* (CBS [Sony Music] CD 62066 [CD], 62066 [LP])

—*Sketches of Spain* (CBS [Sony Music] CD 62327 [CD], 40320223 [C, LP])

DOLPHY, ERIC. *Out to Lunch* (Blue Note 4BN 84163 [C], BST 84163 [LP], CDP 7465242 [CD])

ELLINGTON, DUKE. *Jungle Nights in Harlem* (RCA Bluebird NL 82499 [LP], NK 82499 [C], ND 82499 [CD]). Features Barney Bigard on clarinet.

EVANS, BILL. *At the Village Vanguard* (London Records FCD 60017 [CD])

FITZGERALD, ELLA. *Sings the Duke Ellington Songbook* (Verve [Polygram] 8370352 [CD]). Features Jimmy Hamilton on clarinet.

GETZ, STAN. *Jazz Samba* (Verve [Polygram] 8100611 [LP], 8100612 [CD], 8100614 [C])

—*Stan Getz and Joao Gilberto* (Verve [Polygram] 810048 2 [CD] 230 407 1 [LP])

GIOIA, TED. *The End of the Open Road* (Quartet Q-1001-CD [CD])

—with LEWIS, MARK. *Tango Cool* (Quartet QCD 1006 [CD])

Eddie Daniels

GIUFFRE, JIMMY. *Tangents in Jazz* (Affinity AFF 60 [LP], originally on Capitol)
—*7 Pieces* (Verve 2304 438 [LP])
—*The Jimmy Giuffre 3* (Atlantic Jazz 7 90981-2 [CD])
—*Ad Lib* (Verve 2304 490 [LP])
—*1961* (ECM 849 644-2 [CD])
GOODMAN, BENNY. *King Porter Stomp* (Saville SVL 176 [LP] CSVL 176 [C])
—*Sextet 1939-41 featuring Charlie Christian* (CBS 465679 1 [LP])
—*Live at Carnegie Hall* (CBS 450983 2 [CD], 450983 4 [C])
HALL, EDMOND. *Edmond Hall Quartet* (Storyville 671 190/SLP 190 [LP])
HAMILTON, JIMMY. *It's About Time* (Prestige 0902123 [LP])
JARREAU, AL. *Breakin' Away* (Warner Bros 256917 [CD])
LEWIS, GEORGE. *Sounds of New Orleans Vol. 7: George Lewis and his New Orleans Jazzband* (Storyville SLP 6014)
McFERRIN, BOBBY. *Spontaneous Inventions* (Blue Note CDP 7462982 [CD], BN2 57 [C], BT 85110 [LP])
MINGUS, CHARLES. *Mingus Ah-Um* (CBS [Sony Music] 4504361 [LP], 4504362 [CD], 4504364 [C])
MONK, THELONIOUS. *The Composer* from the Contemporary Jazz Masterpieces series (CBS [Sony Music] 463382 or CK 44297 [CD], 4633384 or CJT 44927 [C/LP])
MORTON, JELLY ROLL. *The Complete Jelly Roll Morton Vol. 1/2* (RCA PM 42 405 [LP]). Features clarinettists Omer Simeon, Barney Bigard and Johnny Dodds.
NICHOLAS, ALBERT. *This is Jazz Vol. 2: Albert Nicholas and the All Star Stompers* (Storyville SLP 4068 [LP])
NOONE, JIMMIE. *Jimmie Noone Volume 1* (Classic Jazz Masters CJM 29 [LP])
PARKER, CHARLIE. *Charlie Parker* in the Compact Jazz and Walkman Jazz series (Verve [Polygram] 8332882 [CD] 8332884 [C])
—*Bird Symbols* (Rhapsody [President] RHCD 5 [CD], RHAP 5 [LP]). These are reissues of the famous Dial recordings.
—*The Best of Bird on Savoy* (Vogue VG655 650109 [CD])
PEPPER, ART. *Landscape* (Galaxy GXY-5128 [LP]). Alto saxophonist Art Pepper plays clarinet on one track.
ROLLINS, SONNY. *Prestige Years Vol. 2 (1954-1956)* (Prestige PRE 4002 [CD])
RUSSELL, PEE WEE. *Ask Me Now* (Impulse A-96 [LP])
SCOTT, TONY. *Golden Moments* (Muse 5230 [LP]). With Bill Evans on piano.
SHAW, ARTIE. *The Complete Gramercy Five Sessions* (RCA Bluebird NL 87637 [LP], NK 87637 [C], ND 87637 [CD])
—*Blues in the Night* (NK 82432 [C], NL 82432 [LP], ND 82432 [CD])
SILVER, HORACE. *Blowin' the Blues Away* (Blue Note/EMI BN2 89/CDP 7465262 [CD], 4BN 84017 [C], BST 84017 [LP])
TATUM, ART. *The Group Masterpieces* (Pablo PACD 2405-430-2). Features Buddy DeFranco on clarinet.
YOUNG, LESTER. *The Lester Young Story Vol. 3: Enter the Count* (CBS 88266 [LP]). Features Lester on clarinet on a couple of tracks.

ee Wee Russell

Mention should also be made of the series of play-along CDs, records and cassettes produced by the American jazz educator **Jamey Aebersold**. There are, at the time of writing, 56 of these featuring compositions by great jazz musicians and also many excellent 'standard' tunes. The records come complete with a booklet which includes melody, chord-progressions and sometimes lyrics. The booklets also sometimes include helpful advice on improvisation. The recordings feature a rhythm section of bass, drums and piano which provides a backing track for you to play the tune and then improvise. These rhythm sections are made up of professional jazz musicians, often among the finest players in the world. Vol. 2 *Nothin' But The Blues* and Vol. 5 *Time To Play Music* are particularly suitable for students moving on from this book.

MOUTHPIECES AND REEDS

The mouthpiece has a crucial effect on the tone quality and ease of playing. The right mouthpiece on a student model instrument will invariably produce better results than the wrong one on an expensive clarinet. Let us then consider the factors which have a major bearing on mouthpiece performance.

Tip opening

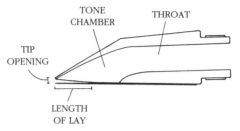

Fig. 24 *Side-view of clarinet mouthpiece.*

The wider the opening, the more effort is required to make the reed vibrate, since it has further to travel. Wide tip openings usually require softer reeds, and narrow openings require harder reeds.

Length of lay

A longer lay will make for easier blowing, but if it is too long it may make tuning difficult to control.

Tone chamber

A bigger chamber produces a rounder sound, a smaller chamber a more brilliant sound.

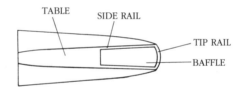

Fig. 25 *Diagram of mouthpiece as viewed from underneath.*

Baffle

The baffle is the slightly raised area near the mouthpiece tip. A high baffle will produce a more 'edgy' sound than a lower one.

Rails

The rails should be straight and not much thicker than one millimetre at the thinnest point. However, ultra-thin rails are likely to encourage tonal instability and squeaks.

When purchasing a mouthpiece examine it carefully to see how well finished it is. It should be perfectly symmetrical. Check that the rails begin to curve at exactly the same point and that the table (Fig. 25) is completely flat. Be cautious. Many modern mouthpieces, even expensive ones, are poorly finished.

It would not be advisable to spend too much money on your first mouthpiece, in case it ultimately proves to be unsuitable. Beware of being over-enthusiastic about a mouthpiece which sounds great in the shop—the acoustics are often more flattering than those of your normal practice room. Many dealers will allow you to try a mouthpiece for a week before committing yourself to purchase. You should take advantage of this facility since it can take time to adapt to a different mouthpiece. It is also important to try the new mouthpiece with a variety of reeds.

Reeds

Even a good mouthpiece will produce poor results if the reed is of poor quality, the wrong grade or the incorrect strength. It is not within the scope of this book to discuss reeds in depth but the most pertinent factors are as follows:

Quality

Never use cheap reeds. Vandoren, Rico, La Voz, and Mitchell Lurie are some of the better brand names.

Strength

Most reeds are numbered to indicate strength—the higher the number the harder the reed. La Voz are actually marked in five grades between soft and hard. Beware of making comparisons between different manufacturers, since grading systems vary. Beginners should generally use a medium-soft or medium reed (grades 2-2$\frac{1}{2}$) unless the mouthpiece tip-opening is very narrow, requiring the use of a harder reed, or very wide, in which case you should use a softer reed.

If the reed is too soft the sound will tend to be feeble and reedy and the high notes will be flat and difficult to produce. Tonguing will also be more difficult, since the reed will have less spring in it.

If on the other hand the reed is too hard your sound will be very breathy; your supply of breath will quickly be exhausted and your embouchure will tire rapidly.

Purchase

You should take advantage of the fact that most shops will allow you to examine reeds before purchase. Look for a golden colour in the blade of the reed. White or green tinges mean that the cane was not mature when cut. Dark brown streaks are not a good sign. Hold the reed up to the light. You should reject any which are chipped or cracked. Examine the grain, which should run parallel with the sides of the reed. It is particularly important that the fibres in the centre run all the way to the tip.

APPENDIX

USEFUL ACCESSORIES

Support-strap

Manufactured by the French company Franck Bichon (trademark BG), this considerably relieves the strain on the right thumb and is therefore particularly suitable for young players.

Pull-Through

A pull-through resembles a handkerchief with a small weight attached to one corner by a chord. This is dropped down the bell of the clarinet, which is then inverted, allowing the weight to drop out of the other end so that it can be pulled through. The purpose of the pull-through is to remove moisture from the pads and prolong their life.

Reed Guard

This protects the reeds from being chipped and also keeps them flat and prevents warping.

Mouthpiece Patches

These are placed on top of the mouthpiece. They cushion the teeth against vibration, which is helpful if you have sensitive teeth, make the mouthpiece feel more comfortable and make it easier for you to achieve consistent placement of the teeth.

Thumb-rest Pad

This is a small piece of rubber which fits over the thumb rest and eases the strain on the right thumb.

Watchmakers' Screwdrivers

The screws on clarinets are never overtightened, and therefore even on the best instruments it is possible that they can work loose through playing. Examine your instrument carefully once a week and tighten any loose screws. *Do not overtighten.*

Tuning Fork

It is best to obtain an A = 440 tuning fork, which corresponds to B on B♭ clarinets.

Metronome

Make sure the metronome clicks loudly enough to be heard. This tends to be more of a problem with electronic metronomes than with mechanical ones.

Cork Grease

The 'lip-salve' type containers are better, since they prevent the grease transferring to your fingers and then being deposited on the clarinet keys.

Reedcutter

A useful device for clipping a small amount off a reed which is too soft, thus making it playable.

Cotton Buds

For cleaning in awkward places, e.g. under the rods, around the pillars and on the inside edges of the tone-holes.

CARE OF THE INSTRUMENT

After you have finished playing use a pull-through to clean the inside of the instrument. You should remove the reed, **gently** wipe off excess moisture, and clean the inside of the mouthpiece with a tissue, taking great care not to rub too hard in the area of the baffle and mouthpiece tip.

Where possible you should brush your teeth before playing, especially if you have just eaten. Mouthpieces are an ideal breeding ground for bacteria. It is particularly important not to play immediately after consuming sweetened foods or drinks.

Cork-grease should be sparingly applied whenever the cork on the tenons shows signs of drying out, otherwise it may crack and need replacing.

It is inevitable that deposits will build up on the reed and affect reed performance. I recommend cleaning reeds with an old toothbrush in warm water, taking care to avoid passing the brush across the tip, and always brushing in the direction of the grain. Rinse the reeds in cold water.

Overhauls and repairs should be entrusted only to an experienced clarinet technician.

TRANSPOSITION

Clarinets are transposing instruments. In other words the note you play is not the note that actually sounds. When you play C, the note that sounds is concert pitch B♭.

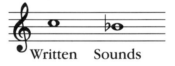

Written   Sounds

As long as you are playing by yourself or with other B♭ clarinets this will not make any difference, but in order to play with concert pitch instruments like piano or guitar, or with instruments pitched in keys other than that of your own clarinet you must **transpose** your music into another key, or they must transpose into your key.

To transpose music written at concert pitch to the correct key you must play a tone higher.

When transposing it is important first to change the key signature, either mentally, if you are simply playing a tune written at concert pitch, or on paper, if you are trying to write it down. This will save you having to think of each note individually. Be careful, however, with accidentals, particularly when applied to the notes B and E. Remember, sharps and flats can transpose to naturals and vice versa. The examples given will illustrate the pitfalls.

FINGERING CHART

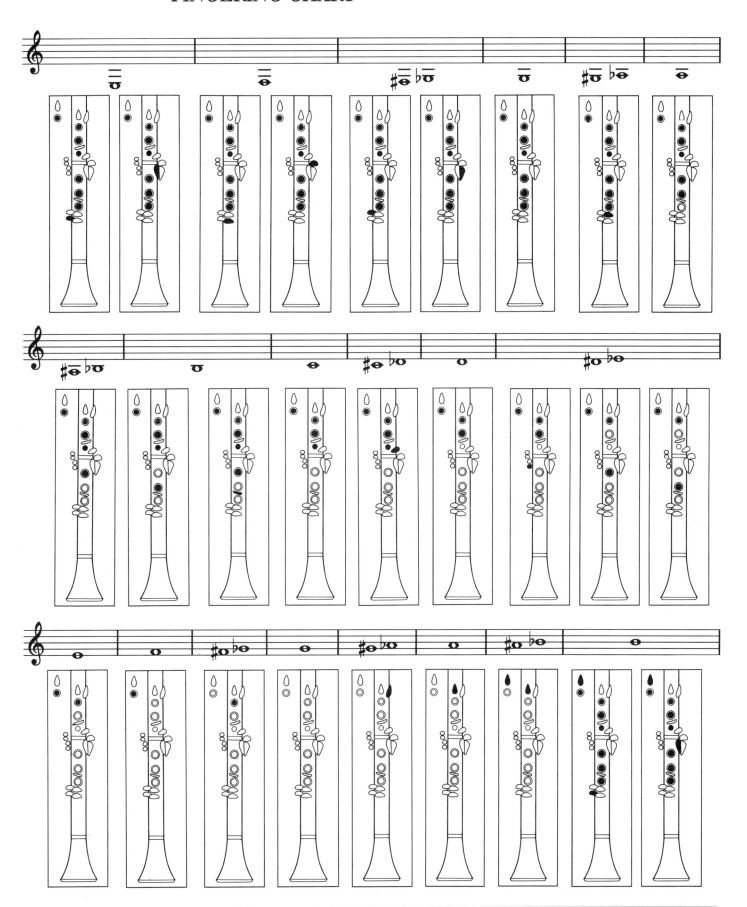

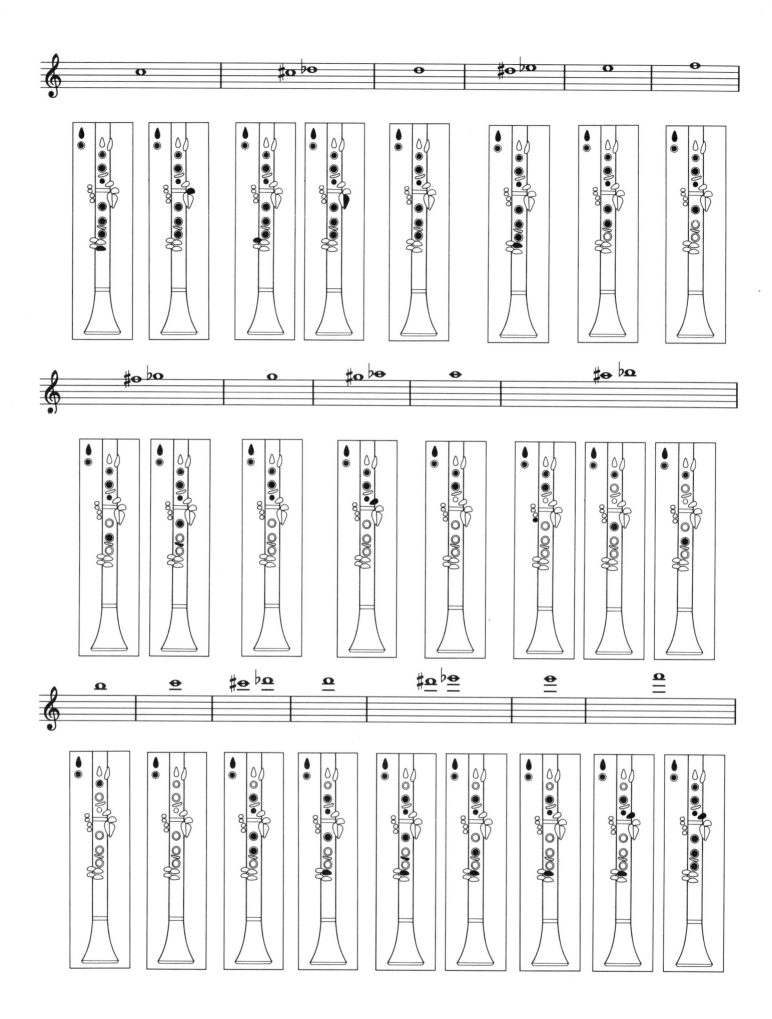

Reproduced and printed by Halstan & Co. Ltd., Amersham, Bucks., England

John O'Neill

The Jazz Method for Clarinet *CD Tracklist*

The Band:
Jimmy Hastings (Clarinet)
Phil Lee (Guitar)
Jeff Clyne (Double Bass)
Paul Clarvis (Drums)
All compositions by John O'Neill unless otherwise indicated

Schott Educational Publications
℗ & © 1995 Schott & Co. Ltd, London
Produced by John O'Neill, Nick Taylor & Wendy Lampa
Sound Engineer: Nick Taylor, Porcupine Studio